Happily Ever Resilient

Happily Ever Resilient

Using Fairy Tales to Nurture Children through Adversity

Stephanie Goloway

Redleaf Press®
www.redleafpress.org
800-423-8309

Published by Redleaf Press
10 Yorkton Court
St. Paul, MN 55117
www.redleafpress.org

First edition 2022

Cover design by Jesse Hughes

Cover photographs and illustrations by Shutterstock

Interior design by Michelle Lee Lagerroos

Typeset in Aglet Slab, DINosaur, and Boucherie Cursive

Interior illustrations by topvectors/stock.adobe.com; Colorlife/stock.adobe.com; Cbetnaha Xap4yk/stock.adobe.com

Printed in the United States of America

29 28 27 26 25 24 23 22   1 2 3 4 5 6 7 8

Library of Congress Cataloging-in-Publication Data
Names: Goloway, Stephanie, author.
Title: Happily ever resilient : using fairy tales to nurture children through adversity / by
    Stephanie Goloway.
Description: First edition. | St. Paul, MN : Redleaf Press, 2022. |
    Includes bibliographical references and index. | Summary: "In Happily Ever Resilient,
    Dr. Stephanie Goloway uses current trauma research and beloved multicultural
    variants of classic children's fairytales to create joyful, playful learning experiences for
    young children"-- Provided by publisher.
Identifiers: LCCN 2021047033 (print) | LCCN 2021047034 (ebook) | ISBN 9781605547442
    (paperback) | ISBN 9781605547459 (ebook)
Subjects: LCSH: Resilience (Personality trait) in children. | Psychic trauma in children. |
    Fairy tales--Study and teaching (Elementary)
Classification: LCC BF723.R46 G65 2022 (print) | LCC BF723.R46 (ebook) |
    DDC 155.4/1824--dc23/eng/20211109
LC record available at https://lccn.loc.gov/2021047033
LC ebook record available at https://lccn.loc.gov/2021047034

Printed on acid-free paper

To my beloved husband, Mike Hospodar, who so longed for hope, "the thing with feathers, that perches in the soul." His wish was that everyone who suffered from trauma and substance use disorders would find it— especially the children.

Contents

Acknowledgments

I am so very grateful to the people who believed this book into being. My deepest gratitude goes to the wonderfully talented Redleaf Press team and especially to my editor and Redleaf fairy godmother, Melissa York, whose shared passion for fairy tales is matched by an exquisite eye for detail and clarity. The late Dr. Darragh Callahan and Dr. Don Yarosz were truly my wizards at Walden University: they asked the tough questions about resilience, executive functions, fairy tales, play, and culture while letting me wander through the magical woods until I found my way to a piece of scholarly research. Don has continued his wizarding long past my graduation date and offered helpful ideas to ensure this book aligns with cutting-edge research while still being accessible and playful.

So many others have been magical helpers along the way. Storyteller and author Gerry Fierst offered his insights into the chapter on fairy tales. Storyteller and author Rafe Martin graciously shared his vast experience and work with folklore to help me wrestle with the issues of cultural integrity in the children's books we highlight. Dr. Dorothy McCall, LCSW, lent her expertise on brain development, trauma, and substance use disorders. TJ McDowell, CAADC, offered insight on substance use disorders. Erin Troup, LPC, NCC, CT, IMH-E IV®, reviewed sections to ensure fidelity to an early childhood mental health perspective. And long ago and far away, Dr. Robert Zanotti and the late Dr. Gordon Hitchings of Edinboro University encouraged my scholarly study of fairy tales in my master's thesis, while the late Piagetian scholar Dr. Jeanette McCarthy Gallagher of Temple University mentored me as I explored representational thinking, play, emergent literacy, and the imagination.

My former students at the Community College of Allegheny County in Pittsburgh helped shape this book through their animated discussions of fairy tales and creative explorations into their use with young children. Special thanks are due to alumnae Harmony Venturino Dudas, Amy Trozzo, Erin Sullivan, Emeline Maslow, Jayme Ranalli, Kathryn Lucia-Faris, Caitlin Hutchinson,

Kalei Smith, and Stephanie Cryor-Gorski for magically finding the time to review and offer constructive feedback on the fairy tale activities as they juggled teaching, families, school, and the challenges of the COVID-19 pandemic.

My friends and former colleagues Kate Stauffer, Suzanne Weathers, Michele Napierkowski, and Dr. Preeti Juneja also all added thoughtful comments and helped to make this book a truly collaborative effort. A huge thank-you is also due to the many children I've learned with over the years—they allowed me to share in their stories and were the sparkling co-creators of many of the activities found in this book.

True magic is the love shared by friends and family. From the sprinkles of positive words and interest from so many, both virtually and in person, to the ongoing positive support of my BFF Karen Cross: I couldn't have done it without you. And mostly, I thank my family. My parents, Phyllis and Ed Goloway, laid the loving foundation to my own resilience, introduced me to fairy tales, and always believed that I would publish a book someday. I am sorry I didn't do it in time for them to celebrate with me. And to my amazing children, Zeke and Jinnie Templin, who put up with a mom who told stories instead of baking them cookies and have cheered me on every slow and halting step of the way: I love you. Here's to the happily-ever-afters you both deserve.

Introduction

A Story about Why We Need This Book

Once upon a time, there was a young woman. She was kind and hardworking, and she had big dreams. One day her mother told her that she must make her way in the world, and so she set off to find her fortune.

The young woman followed her heart to a castle in the forest. As she stood outside, she heard the laughter and play of young children, and it delighted her. Eager to join in, she pounded on the huge castle door.

"Yes???" said the stern woman who answered the door. "Who are you and why have you come?"

"I am but a poor wanderer who heard the joy coming from within your castle walls. Please, may I come in and share in it? I will work hard! I know stories and songs, and I am sure I could help."

The stern woman looked her up and down. "Hummph," she said. "The queen is *very* particular about who may play with the royal children. Come sleep in the guest chamber tonight, and we will see what tomorrow brings."

The grateful young woman followed her hostess through winding, dark hallways and at last was shown a bed piled high with feather mattresses. She climbed up and prepared for a long-overdue night's sleep. She sighed, stretched, and snuggled into the soft covers.

The next morning, she was brought before the Queen. "How did you sleep, fair wanderer?" asked the Queen, looking down from atop a high throne.

The young woman curtsied and bowed and then wrung her hands. "Your Majesty, I was thankful to rest in such a fine royal bed last night. But alas, I did not sleep a wink! There was something large and hard and spikey in the mattress, I'm afraid, and it kept me awake all night!"

The Queen stared at her for a moment, then announced, "You have passed the test. I pronounce you royal caregiver to all the kingdom's children." The Queen rose from her throne and began to walk away.

"Oh, thank you, Queen!" stammered the young woman. "But . . . what was the test? And what was that horrid thing in the bed that kept me tossing and turning all night?"

The Queen looked back over her shoulder. "That was the test to get hired. Your next test is figuring out what it was. Now, quickly: go and prepare your lesson plans so I may review them. The children are about to arrive."

And so the young woman found her heart's path and spent many years learning and playing and singing with the children of the kingdom. There was, however, not a day that went by when she didn't wonder what it was that haunted her sleep and made every day shine just a little less brightly than it could.

Just like the young woman in "The Princess and the Pea," many of us in the early childhood field have struggled to figure out why things are so difficult for some children. Sometimes it's the children who are too loud and boisterous, and sometimes it's the children who sit silently and stare. Sometimes it's the look a child gives us right before pickup time; sometimes it's the way they hold tight around our necks, trying to melt into us. We get this nagging feeling we need to figure it out: a key to unlock a child's learning potential and help them enter our classroom community with laughter and curiosity. It keeps us awake at night, and we worry about what will happen as these children move on into schools and programs that are less child centered than our own.

Needless to say, there is no single key to unlocking every child's mysteries. But we *do* have decades of research on how trauma of various kinds influences young children's development, and many professionals are now connecting the dots between the toxic stress caused by such trauma and a whole host of challenging behaviors we see in the classroom. Could this be the "pea" that makes us toss and turn as we ponder how to meet children's needs?

We also have a great deal of evidence that *resilience* is a primary protective factor against damage caused by many sources of trauma, including natural disasters, war, displacement, racism, community violence, parental incarceration, child abuse, and substance use disorder (alcoholism/addiction). We've learned that we can intentionally nurture this "magic wand" of resilience in young children. Most important, what we know about resilience offers insight into how we, as early childhood professionals, can help.

This book looks at these serious issues and offers early childhood educators two things: (1) evidence-based knowledge about the way trauma affects young children's social-emotional and cognitive development; and (2) playful and developmentally appropriate ways that teachers can integrate the neuro-protective factors of resilience into their child-centered, literacy-rich curricula through fairy tales and storytelling.

Understanding trauma is hard work emotionally and intellectually. But supporting children as they develop their ability to bounce back from adversity—their resilience—can be a joyful and rich experience that draws on the best of what we know about developmentally appropriate practice. The ideas in this book will help you polish up the sparkling strategies you already use in your classroom so you can intentionally create a classroom community that nurtures resilience while fostering learning. *All* children deserve the tools to fight off whatever dragons they encounter as they move through life. And we, as early childhood educators, can be the fairy godmothers and godfathers who provide them with those tools.

Part One:
Ordinary Magic for Challenging Times

The
Ordinary Magic
of Resilience

So what is resilience? For years *resilience* described a person's ability to bounce back from traumatic events. Researchers believed that some individuals were born with this extraordinary capacity, which came to light only when they experienced adversity. Tales of exceptional people overcoming tremendous odds and having happy and successful lives after tragedy shaped what most of us knew about resilience.

But in recent decades, researchers like Dr. Ann Masten (2015) and others have discovered that resilience is actually "ordinary magic"—that is, it is a neurodevelopmental capacity that *all* of us can have. It develops through the common interactions and experiences of childhood; scholars point to it as the primary protective factor for healthy outcomes in adulthood. No matter our socioeconomic status, education, or birth family, we all encounter stressful life challenges, and resilience is what allows us to move forward to the next challenge and adventure.

What does this have to do with early childhood educators? As we'll be discussing, educators matter a lot! By turning our focus to developing this powerful force in children's lives, we are laying the foundation for their future academic, social, and life success. We can transform our best practices surrounding play, stories, and nurturing relationships into the protective factors for resilience: attachment, initiative, self-regulation, and cultural affirmation.

Developing resilience is important for *all* children. We often don't know for sure which children face stressful home situations. We identify and are frustrated by challenging behaviors, but we don't know what the root causes—or solutions—are. And when we direct our attention to children who are having a tough time, we wonder whether we are taking away time from children who sit quietly and demand little. We are overwhelmed with fulfilling state learning standards and local expectations while still meeting the needs of children desperate for attention, support, and guidance.

To understand why resilience is such an essential tool in our magic bag of tricks, we first need to understand trauma and toxic stress and how they affect young children's development. Like resilience, these concepts are best viewed from the perspective of brain development and the way it translates into children's behaviors. It's not enough to know that child abuse, domestic violence, and addiction can derail children's development and cause challenging behaviors. We've known that for years. Understanding *how* these adverse childhood experiences affect the brains of young children gives us hope, since resilience is such a perfect match for what growing brains need.

The Trauma Dragon

To better understand how we can support resilience in a classroom, let's look at some of the specific hurdles facing children who have experienced trauma and other life challenges that disrupt family systems. These experiences are known as adverse childhood experiences, or ACEs (American Academy of Pediatrics 2014). ACEs were first identified and examined in 1997 by the Centers for Disease Control and Prevention (CDC) as part of a landmark study of 17,000 middle-income adults, conducted in conjunction with Kaiser-Permanente (Felitti et al. 1998). ACEs include life events such as physical and sexual abuse, living with parental substance use disorder, divorce, and domestic or community violence. This cluster of experiences, individually or collectively, has often been found to negatively affect children's development, as well as their long-term physical and mental health outcomes.

The Truth about ACEs

How Prevalent Are ACEs?

The ACE study revealed the following estimates:

Abuse

Physical Abuse	28.3%
Sexual Abuse	20.7%
Emotional Abuse	10.6%

(percentage of study participants who experienced a specific ACE)

Neglect

Emotional Neglect	14.8%
Physical Neglect	9.9%

Household Dysfunction

Household Substance Abuse	26.9%
Parental Divorce	23.3%
Household Mental Illness	19.4%
Mother Treated Violently	12.7%
Incarcerated Household Member	4.7%

Robert Wood Johnson Foundation, 2013

Possible Risk Outcomes

Behavior				
Lack of physical activity	Smoking	Alcoholism	Drug use	Missed work
Physical & Mental Health				
Severe obesity	Diabetes	Depression	Suicide attempts	STDs
Heart disease	Cancer	Stroke	COPD	Broken bones

No one working in education needs a crystal ball to identify these factors: we have all seen the effects on children. However, what was most significant about the CDC study were revelations about how common these experiences are and their long-term effect. The number of ACEs a child experiences is directly related to adult mental health challenges such as anxiety and depression, as well as an increased likelihood of developing a substance use disorder. More surprisingly, a person's ACE score is also connected with an increased risk for cardiovascular disease and chronic health issues such as diabetes (American Academy of Pediatrics 2014). Traumatic events literally get under our skin and affect our physical and mental health for the rest of our lives.

When early childhood educators are aware of challenging home situations (or guess that they are occurring), it's easy to attribute children's challenging behaviors to poor role models and a lack of limit setting. However, neuroscience offers another explanation. Toxic stress, which occurs under chronic or severe adversity, has been found to interrupt healthy brain architecture in young children, affecting parts of the brain most directly responsible for emotional regulation and executive functions (National Scientific Council on the Developing Child [2005] 2014).

We'll be discussing emotional regulation and executive functions in-depth throughout this book. For now, it may help to think of the child who can't sit still during circle time or stay focused on the steps of a routine like hand washing. These children appear to face challenges with self-regulation and executive functions. While the source of these behaviors in an individual might be something other than toxic stress, research encourages us to take a deeper look at such behaviors from a trauma-informed perspective.

The Trauma Dragon's Flames: Toxic Stress

High school biology and health classes teach that stress is part of a normal, healthy response pattern. When we notice something is different or unexpected, our brains go into high-alert mode to make sure we stay safe and activate the fight, flight, or freeze stress-response system to keep us out of danger. So, the example goes, when our cave-dwelling ancestors saw a saber-tooth tiger, their stress response kicked into high gear. The limbic system, which controls emotions like fear, communicated directly with the brain stem, which controls breathing, heart rate, and various survival mechanisms. They didn't stand around evaluating solutions with their prefrontal cortex, the part of the brain where executive functions and decision-making are rooted. Instead, with all physical systems turned up, our ancestors' hearts rapidly pumped blood to their extremities, their lungs filled with air, and they hightailed out of there.

This worked for our ancestors. Encounters with saber-tooth tigers were relatively rare. After our ancestors escaped the tiger, their heart rates, breathing, and adrenaline surges returned to normal, and they calmed down and went about their business. We can assume that this response system worked for knights battling dragons for the same reason. However, when this same stress response system activates in our twenty-first-century world, it is often not because of physical danger. Low-level chronic stress, such as dealing with a challenging job or living through a pandemic that puts changing expectations and limitations on us, can result in the physiological response of toxic stress.

So then two things happen. First, there is no physical outlet for all the energy surging through our bodies. Our ancestors used their pumping hearts to run fast, but we usually do not need to. Second, there often is not enough time for our bodily systems and brains to return to normal before our stress response is triggered again. Many sources of modern-day stress, such as cranky coworkers, commutes with traffic, or watching the news, are ongoing, constant parts of our lives.

This is also true for young children living with domestic violence, abuse, or inconsistent and nonresponsive parenting. Their bodily systems and brains don't return to normal before the stress response activates again. Over time they develop hypervigilance: their limbic systems and their fight, flight, freeze responses are always on. They tend to be reactive (more likely to overrespond to being bumped or getting left out of a game, for example), and their prefrontal cortex and self-regulatory systems don't have the chance to develop as efficiently as they should. Hence, many have poor self-regulation and diminished executive function skills (National Scientific Council on the Developing Child 2005/2014).

A lack of self-regulation and executive function influences children's ability to form relationships, solve problems, and learn. These activities are critical to being part of a supportive classroom community, and all contribute to the "ordinary magic" of resilience. Further, the brain systems involved with the stress response and self-regulation are implicated in the development of substance use disorders (Volkow et al. 2014). In other words, without positive experiences that promote executive functions and self-regulation, these children are at greater risk of substance use disorder in adolescence and adulthood than others are, since their brains are structurally more vulnerable.

Some researchers note that children who experience challenging family situations have limited access to friendships in their home settings as well. They attribute this to many factors, including parental shame, undesirable living conditions, and children's desire to protect the family from outsiders as they get older (Moe 2019). Children bring this lack of experience in making and keeping friends into the classroom setting. Childhood friendships are important both for engaging in the learning process and for developing social skills. Brown (2014) offered evidence that peer interactions may compensate for even severe lack of caring adult interaction. His case study with severely abused and neglected orphans in Romania demonstrated that through therapeutic playwork, the children made social and emotional gains that he would not have predicted based on their adverse experiences. Brown attributed the gains to the social connections children formed with peers, which allowed them to interact when adult clinicians and playworkers were not present.

Developing self-regulation requires *co-regulation*, or sensitive interactions with a tuned-in caregiver (Murray et al. 2015). Beginning with the serve-and-return, or back-and-forth dialogues, that occur every time a baby says "aaah" and the caregiver says "aaah" back, co-regulation includes helping children identify their emotions and creating an environment that supports self-regulation. For example, a toddler clenches her fists and scrunches her face. Co-regulation occurs when her father says, "What's the matter, honey? You look frustrated. Is your princess gown buried in the toy box?" and then places the gown, or an

alternative, within reach. This kind of tuning in to children's emergent language and their emotional states is often absent when parents are experiencing adversity themselves, such as domestic violence or substance use. Therefore, it's not surprising that children living with ACEs are at a higher risk for challenges with self-regulation.

Many studies identify a relationship between self-regulation and academic success. The National Institute for Early Education Research (NIEER) recommends that all early childhood programs include a focus on social and emotional development, including self-regulation (Friedman-Krauss and Barnett 2013). Blair and Raver (2015) reviewed numerous studies on the relationship between self-regulation and school readiness in young children, spanning diverse socioeconomic, geographic, and ethnic populations. They concluded that "an approach to the promotion of school readiness by fostering the development of self-regulation offers the potential to remake early education in a way that is effective for all children" (724).

These researchers advocate for a both/and approach to self-regulation and pre-academics in preschool, based on evidence that when children are prepared with social and emotional skills, emergent literacy and math competencies improve. Early childhood educators who understand developmentally appropriate practice have been saying this for decades! We *know* that relationships are the core of a quality early care and education program and that these relationships are developed through play, conversation, and shared experiences. Yet we often have to fight to convince people that these rich child-centered practices deserve equal time with pursuits that look more academic. This is especially true in classrooms where children are seen to be academically at risk because of their home learning environments. Teachers may believe that more academics and less play is the best way to prepare these children for future school challenges. However, research strongly suggests that focusing on social and emotional development is even *more* important to children living in adverse conditions, including poverty (Center on the Developing Child 2016). Brain science and resilience to the rescue!

A Special Kind of Dragon: Family Substance Use Disorder

Many researchers have examined the negative impact of family substance use disorder (SUD) on children. Both the ACEs study (American Academy of Pediatrics 2014) and the National Scientific Council on the Developing Child ([2008] 2012) identified living with SUD as one of the major sources of toxic stress in children. SUD is also one of the largest public health crises facing the United States, although this was eclipsed in our national discussion in 2020 and 2021 by the global pandemic. The pandemic itself has resulted in increases in the incidence of SUDs and overdose deaths (American Medical Association 2021).

In the fifth edition of the *Diagnostic and Statistical Manual of Mental Disorders (DSM-5)*, the American Psychiatric Association (2013) defines SUD as a mental disorder involving characteristic cognitive, behavioral, and physiological symptoms that contribute to an individual continuing the use of one or more substances (alcohol, opioids, stimulants, hallucinogens, and so on) despite significant social, psychological, physical, or economic consequences. Previous DSM editions used other names, including alcoholism and addiction.

While some don't tend to think of substance use as an issue of early childhood (except perhaps for fetal alcohol syndrome), early childhood caregivers concerned about trauma need to know several things about the disease:

- **It is estimated that one in four children lives in a home affected by SUD**. The disease cuts across socioeconomic, age, and gender categories. While the parent who rushes in to pick up their child smelling like beer may be suffering from the disease, so might the college professor or doctor who is always on time. Alcoholism has seen as much of an increase in the first two decades of the twenty-first century as opioid addiction has (Grant et al. 2017).

- **Most clinicians, doctors, and researchers support the disease model of SUD**. It is treated as a progressive, chronic, and potentially fatal disease of the brain, resulting in physical changes to the brain's structure (Volkow and Koob 2015). This physiological understanding of SUD highlights the critical importance of early childhood experiences that support healthy brain architecture in areas key to the later prevention of SUD.

- **The disease of SUD is determined in large part by genetics**. Children who have at least one biological parent who suffers from the disease are between two and ten times more likely to develop the disease as adolescents or adults compared to their peers who do not have a parent with the genetic predisposition (Solis et al. 2012). This makes SUD more heritable than most cancers, diabetes, and cardiovascular disease, all of which we accept may "run in families."

- **Substance use disorder is rarely the only ACE in homes where it is present**. Because of the way it affects thinking, behavior, and self-regulation, children living in homes with family SUD experience a much higher rate of abuse, neglect, and family disruptions such as divorce and

incarcerations than other children. Between 40 and 80 percent of cases brought to child protection services involve at least one caregiver suffering from the disease (Solis et al. 2012).

- **Parents and caregivers who have SUD love their children, and if willpower was all it took, they would be in recovery.** This is perhaps one of the hardest facts for those of us who love children to grapple with: If the parents care, why don't they do whatever it takes to get better? While this seems like a reasonable question, it's important to wonder whether we would ask the same question of someone with cancer or another serious disease. For the person without a SUD, it's pretty clear-cut: stop drinking. Just as we would not expect someone with cancer to will away their cancer cells, it is not fair to expect someone with SUD to will away the chemistry of their brain. However, it is this type of overhaul that's required for someone with this disease to refrain from drinking or using drugs. Recovery is a sophisticated, lengthy, costly, and challenging process, which, like type 1 diabetes, is ongoing for the rest of one's life.

- **Attachment is especially problematic for many young children living with SUD.** In addition to inconsistent or absent parenting, parents and caregivers with SUD are less likely to have the social network of support that buffers the normal stress of parenting infants and young children (Harper Browne 2014). The added stress of parenting with SUD, whether under the influence of drugs or alcohol or dealing with the cognitive and emotional impact of the disease, lessens the opportunities to nurture healthy attachment relationships with young children (Lander, Howsare, and Byrne 2013). Further, when a parent is in treatment or incarcerated, or the child is placed in foster care due to parental negligence or abuse, attachment bonds may be damaged (Conners-Burrow et al. 2013; National Institute on Drug Abuse 2021).

- **Lower self-regulation skills and more challenging behaviors, as well as higher incidences of depression and anxiety, are often found in children living with SUD** (Eiden et al. 2009; Lander, Howsare, and Byrne 2013). As discussed previously, such challenging behaviors harm the child's ability to form positive relationships in a child care or school setting, especially when teachers do not feel they have the background or resources to deal with the behaviors in a group setting (Onchwari 2010). When combined with the stigma that children sometimes face when their teachers know that a parent is addicted to drugs or alcohol (Conners-Burrow et al. 2013), it may also be more difficult for children living with SUD to form healthy attachments with their teachers than it is for them to do so with other children.

● **It is important to recognize the strengths children and families demonstrate as they adapt to challenging circumstances.** Each family affected by SUD is unique. In addition to the ordinary factors that make families different, with SUD, there are differences in the substances used, the temperaments of the adults and children affected, and the severity of the disease. These contribute to the varied coping strategies children learn and bring into the classroom. The classic alcoholic family roles—the hero, the scapegoat, the lost child, and the mascot/clown—can seem dysfunctional when viewed out of context in the early childhood classroom (Ackerman 1987). However, each child and family deserves our individual attention and respect as we learn from the ways they cope, so we can provide an environment of healthy relationships in which they can grow.

The preceding sections on trauma, toxic stress, and substance use disorders tell a sad and frightening story indeed. But, as all fairy tale lovers know, with strength, wisdom, bravery, and the right kind of magic, no quest is too challenging! Researcher and longtime early childhood advocate Ellen Galinsky surveyed the tremendous amount of information on trauma and trauma-informed care from the 2010s. We now recognize the effects ACEs have on young children's brain development and why. Yet Galinsky and others in the field believe it is important to change the narrative surrounding childhood trauma. Too often, they say, we become overwhelmed with the enormity of the challenge and focus on the deficits that many children bring into our classrooms. Instead, we should think about the assets children and families bring and the positive childhood experiences (PCEs) they have that we can share with them (O'Connor 2020). Galinsky (2020) states, "Adversity is not destiny!" (47). Resilience is the magic potion that can neutralize toxic stress and support the next generation of brave adventurers.

Resilience: The Ordinary Magic

So what are the secret ingredients in this magical elixir of resilience? Researchers have scrutinized why some children who experience trauma have far better outcomes than others. These studies focus on *relationships* and *resilience* as primary protective factors against toxic stress (for example, National Scientific Council on the Developing Child 2015; Ronel and Levy-Cahana 2011).

Harvard's National Scientific Council on the Developing Child analyzed multiple research studies from a variety of perspectives, including the field of brain development. The council compiled a set of key factors that build resilience, including the following:

- a relationship with at least one stable, caring, and supportive adult
- a sense of control over circumstances
- strong executive function and self-regulation skills
- a supportive faith and/or cultural context (National Scientific Council on the Developing Child 2015)

There is significant overlap between the skills commonly described as social-emotional learning (SEL) and the protective factors of resilience. Gartrell and Cairone (2014) define *resilience* as "the ability to use social-emotional skills to overcome, or bounce back from, the effects of stress in one's life" (92). The actual protective factors for resilience have been studied and described very specifically by Dr. Masten and others, and an in-depth examination of these is useful for early childhood educators. As can be seen in the table below, all of these identified protective factors are inherent in the developmentally appropriate practices that underpin high-quality early care and education.

Resilience Factors with ECE Examples (adapted from Masten 2015)

Resilience Factors	Examples in the Early Childhood Classroom
Effective caregiving and quality parenting	Teacher rocks and soothes child after he scrapes knee on playground.
Close relationships with other capable adults	Teachers and assistants spend time laughing and talking with children during lunch, assisting with opening juice boxes.
Close friends and romantic partners	Children choose who they wish to play with during center time and are encouraged to give each other notes and pictures.
Intelligence and problem-solving skills	Children have long periods of time in the construction area so they can figure out how to build a bridge like the one they saw in "The Three Billy Goats Gruff."
Self-control; emotion regulation; planfulness	Classroom has short, engaging circle times that include movement and yoga to help children calm their bodies.
Motivation to succeed	Teachers and other children scaffold a child's attempts to climb up the slide ladder by offering feedback, waiting patiently, and being encouraging.
Self-efficacy	Children are given trays of interesting loose parts and encouraged to invent something they would like to play with and then asked to share their wonderful ideas.
Faith, hope, belief life has meaning	The classroom has a ritual where each child is greeted with a secret handshake by a teacher and two other children each morning.

The Ordinary Magic of Relationships

Harvard's Center on the Developing Child joins generations of theorists, researchers, and practitioners in affirming that the single most important thing that can positively affect a child's development is a stable relationship with at least one caring and supportive adult (National Scientific Council on the Developing Child 2015). Often called *attachment*, this relationship is ideally with the child's primary caregiver and starts at birth. Advances in neuroscience have given us more specific information about the serve-and-return responses between a child and caregiver and how they wire the brain for later relationship building and emotional maturity.

Children living in challenging family situations sometimes lack this kind of stable relationship with a parent. Masten (2015) discusses how this relationship can also form with another competent adult: a family member such as a grandparent, a child care provider, or a close neighbor, for example. As children get older, these relationships with other competent adults become more important and contribute significantly to the child's resilience.

A child's relationship with peers also contributes to resilience. This includes siblings, playmates, best friends, and romantic partners in adolescence and adulthood. As discussed previously, children experiencing family SUD and other ACEs sometimes have fewer opportunities to forge these relationships, especially in the home setting, which makes it crucial that the early childhood classroom provides children with many opportunities to establish and explore friendships.

In fact, the early childhood classroom is the ideal place to foster all of these relationships. Teachers act as surrogate caregivers for the majority of a child's day, especially for younger children. When these teacher-child relationships are prioritized because of the role they play in fostering resilience, children thrive. Through one-on-one relationships, teachers also gain important developmental information to support children's self-regulation and their learning in more traditional pre-academic areas.

Teachers, support staff, administrators, and other adults in the center or school can all provide children with stable and caring relationships that nurture resilience. Practices as simple as welcoming each child by name or knowing a child's favorite lunch food invite children to see the world of adults as a source of support and have demonstrated benefits for children's long-term social-emotional and cognitive development (Howell and Reinhard 2015).

Similarly, the research on resilience highlights how children benefit from lots of time to collaborate with each other (Nicolopoulou et al. 2015). Whether playing out scenes from a favorite story on the playground or working together to solve a tricky math problem, interacting with peers allows children to develop

the relationship-building skills that are critical for resilience. Skills like social problem solving, perspective taking, and conflict resolution take time and practice to develop, and supportive classrooms enhance every child's chances for a resilient future.

The Ordinary Magic of Initiative

Initiative is an umbrella term that describes children's ability to use their own ideas to act on and control their environment. This aspect of resilience, which Masten (2015) calls *mastery motivation*, encompasses traits like agency, self-efficacy, and motivation to succeed. In young children, initiative includes skills and dispositions such as trying new activities, showing an interest in learning new things, using different ways to solve a problem, and showing confidence in their abilities (LeBuffe and Naglieri 2012).

Responsive caregivers provide children with opportunities to act on their environments and gain new skills in a supported yet autonomous way, helping them develop their sense of self-empowerment. This is critical to the development of a child's sense of agency, which "arises from the experience of overcoming manageable challenges and a robust sense of self-efficacy [that] in turn fosters persistence in the face of adversity, which is more likely to lead to success than giving up" (Masten 2015, 161). This persistence is important for all children, but especially for those whose home experiences have not offered them the encouragement or opportunity to keep trying when things get hard.

While many of the behaviors that demonstrate initiative overlap with executive functions (discussed below), Masten (2015) emphasizes that the joy and satisfaction young children experience when they make things happen in their environments are essential components of this aspect of resilience. A cornerstone of child-centered and emergent curriculum practices, initiative has been challenging for teachers to preserve as they navigate the waves of accountability and ever-earlier standardized assessment. The perfect context for initiative is play, which by definition is self-motivated and child directed. But offering children the chance to follow their own wonderful ideas, as Eleanor Duckworth (2006) called them, means teachers have to give up some control over children's activity in the classroom. From a practical standpoint, assessing a child's math thinking as they are creating a self-designed castle takes more time and effort than using a worksheet to do so. Hopefully, understanding why initiative is such an important aspect of resilience may help us to reprioritize play and embrace more open-ended assessment strategies.

The Ordinary Magic of Executive Functions

Giving children lots of time to come up with their own problems and solve them in the context of play also supports a related protective factor for resilience— *executive functions*. Executive functions (EFs) are a cluster of cognitive skills based primarily in the prefrontal cortex of the brain, which is responsible for the processes we call thinking. Dr. Adele Diamond, a leading researcher on executive functions in children, has identified three primary EFs: inhibitory control (related to self-regulation), working memory (being able to keep relevant information in mind while working on tasks), and cognitive flexibility (being able to see things from different perspectives and find multiple solutions to a problem). These lay the foundation for other higher-order thinking skills and affect all areas of cognitive and social functioning (Diamond 2014).

Executive functions arise in early childhood and continue developing through middle childhood, adolescence, and early adulthood. They are central to school success, life success, and resilience. Adult tasks such as being able to hold a job, maintain a romantic relationship, and figure out what to do when your computer won't start all have their roots in EFs, as do things such as inventing driverless cars and analyzing data from Mars. Like other aspects of resilience, EFs develop through engaging experiences and interactions. While research is still uncovering specific experiences that may be most conducive to their development, pretend play and storytelling have both been identified as promoting EFs (Center on the Developing Child 2016).

Think of a group of preschoolers playing castle. They are using *working memory* to hold in mind who is the princess, the king, the baby, and the royal dog and to maintain their roles: the "dog" has to remember to crawl, "bark talk," and not use their hands when eating from their bowl. *Cognitive flexibility* comes into play when they decide to have pizza for dinner but there is no corresponding play food. Do they switch to the plastic burgers and fries in the fridge? Or do they pretend the plates in the dramatic play area are "personal pan pizzas"? Or does one of them retrieve construction paper from the art area and make a large paper pizza? When the child playing the "dog" stops themselves from reaching for the "pizza" on the table, they are using *inhibitory control*, or self-regulation. Inhibitory control is at the heart of resolving conflicts as children are co-constructing a story. Do I insist that I am the princess and I am going to wear the blue cape, or do I let the king wear it, like he wants to? What if I decide I don't want to be the dog and want to be the knight, but they say no, there isn't a knight? Do I stay the dog, and keep the story going, or do I leave and go to the block area? Decisions like these that occur in the micro-interactions of pretend play are why famed

psychologist Lev Vygotsky (1978) said that in make-believe, children are "a head taller than themselves." In other words, they exhibit more mature self-regulation and reasoning skills because they have a strong incentive to keep the story going.

The Ordinary Magic of Self-Regulation

Few aspects of a child's development have a more immediate impact on the classroom than self-regulation. Sometimes called self-control, self-regulation is the ability to manage one's emotions and actions and is considered a key indicator for success in school (Center on the Developing Child 2011). The child who cannot sit still during circle time, who cannot stop themselves from shoving the child who bumps into their block castle, or who bursts into tears when another child takes their crayon is challenged by self-regulation. Indeed, all young children are still developing this protective factor for resilience.

Children with certain temperaments are more prone to self-regulation challenges, as are children who have been exposed to toxic stress. Even the relatively minor stressors of being tired or hungry can reduce one's ability to self-regulate, at least temporarily. Just think of your own response to a toddler's "why" questions if you didn't get much sleep the night before, compared to your response on days when you feel refreshed. Research on stress and self-regulation applies to adults as well as to children.

The Ordinary Magic of Cultural Context and Affirmation

The fourth protective factor for resilience is the feeling we get when we are part of something bigger than ourselves (National Scientific Council on the Developing Child 2015). Spiritual and cultural traditions are cited as the most common ways this factor is provided for children. However, routines, traditions, and rituals in the early childhood classroom can be a source of this affirmation as well (Howell and Reinhard 2015).

It is central to best practices in early education that we honor each child's home culture in our classrooms. Additionally, Howell and Reinhard (2015) offer insight into the culture of the classroom, school, and center, considering how educators can intentionally include children in affirming and wonderful practices. Whether it is singing a special song to mark the end of playtime, bringing out certain magical materials to play with only at the very end of the day, or celebrating "Pizza Friday," early educators can use classroom routines and strategies to provide a consistent cultural context that lets all children know they are part of a vibrant and positive community of learners.

Many of the suggestions found in this book place classroom routines and activities within the broader cultural context of fairy tales. As we'll see, helping children make connections within the universal web of Story can promote this sense of belonging while fostering other aspects of resilience as well.

The National Scientific Council on the Developing Child (2015) and the Center on the Developing Child (2016) recommend that we all view early childhood education as an important component of societal efforts to promote resilience in all children. While educators cannot mediate the parent-child relationship, we can provide children with supplemental adult and peer relationships as well as experiences that promote self-efficacy, self-regulation, and executive function skills. In the next chapters, we'll be looking at how educators can use play, fairy tales, and storytelling to construct an enriching and challenging curriculum that fosters the protective factors of resilience for all children.

Discover More

The Center for the Developing Child at Harvard University has a wide range of resources on resilience, executive function, self-regulation, toxic stress, and other important concepts related to child development (see https://developingchild .harvard.edu/science/key-concepts/).

The Center for the Developing Child also offers a guide for activities that develop executive function skills for age groups from infants through adolescents at https://developingchild .harvard.edu/resources/activities-guide-enhancing-and -practicing-executive-function-skills-with-children-from -infancy-to-adolescence.

For more information about Ann Masten's "ordinary magic," we recommend her video presentation titled "Inside Resilient Children" at https://www.youtube.com/watch?time_continue=2&v =GBMet8oIvXQ.

Sesame Street Community puts children's favorite characters to work addressing tough topics, many of which (such as parental substance use disorders, incarceration, homelessness, divorce, grief, and violence) are related to ACEs. Each topic features videos to share with children, along with resources including lesson plans, articles, and parent-friendly fact sheets. Developed in conjunction with experts on child development, trauma, and resilience, this is a valuable tool to add to your treasure chest: https://sesamestreetincommunities.org/topics/.

The Extraordinary Magic of Fairy Tales

Fairy tales have gone in and out of favor for centuries, according to renowned folklorist and author Jane Yolen. The fairy tale haters arrive, she writes, with a rhythmic regularity, and "under the banner of reason, they blast away with their howitzer at the little singing bird of faerie" (Yolen [1981] 2005, 49).

In the 1960s and 1970s, parents and teachers revolted against the age-old stories because of their violence as well as the anti-feminist princesses waiting passively to be rescued by the prince. More recently, there have been concerns about age discrimination (why are old women always witches?) and how "true love's kiss" awakens Snow White and Sleeping Beauty without their consent. We also question whether traditional tales from Indigenous cultures around the world can be told authentically by storytellers and authors who were not raised in those cultures.

While there are valid concerns about some versions of the tales, including those made popular by animators and filmmakers, the fact remains that children continue to love these age-old tales of magic from all over the world. They persist in bringing the stories' original ancient themes into their play and storytelling despite well-meaning adults trying to protect them.

Why is this? To better understand the continuing power of fairy tales in the twenty-first century, we look to theory; to the practical experience of veteran teacher Vivian Paley; to cutting-edge research about neuroscience and resilience; and to the storytellers, whose lifework it is to preserve our cultural heritage. When all of these are taken together, we have a compelling rationale for bringing this classic form of folk literature into our early childhood classrooms. We have new reasons to trust the children's instincts that the magic of fairy tales is benevolent and good—and that it can help them grow happily ever resilient, no matter what dragons they are currently battling.

Fairy Tales, Magical Thinking, and Representation

One theory that provides a foundation for developmentally effective practice comes from Jean Piaget. Piaget helped us understand how very different the thinking of young children is from our adult logic (Cohen and Waite-Stupiansky 2017). He investigated the specifics of why this is so and demonstrated the importance of active learning: it is only through acting on their environment that children develop logical thinking so they can understand the world as an orderly and systematic place. Until this gradually happens during their early elementary school years, children engage in what Piaget called *magical thinking*. Quite simply, children believe in magic because they have not yet constructed the mental schemes to understand causality in the physical and social worlds.

For example, a young child drops a ball and it bounces. He then drops a rock and it thuds. The explanation why does not lie with the law of physics for the child. Instead, perhaps the ball is more alive than the rock and *wants* to jump around and please the child, just like the magical objects and creatures in fairy tales. Piaget called this tendency of children to give human characteristics to toys, rocks, and other nonliving objects *animism*. Piaget's concept of animism is one way the magical thinking of young children mirrors the magic in fairy tales (1962).

This magic defines fairy tales, according to the scholars who study them. "The Three Bears" and "The Three Little Pigs" aren't fairy tales, strictly speaking, since they don't contain magic. But like most familiar fairy tales, these folktales come from the oral tradition, passed down by storytellers for centuries. They are favorites of children because they have talking animals, straightforward plots, and clear-cut distinctions between what happens to the good and bad characters. These characteristics also align with young children's cognitive development according to Piaget (1965).

Piaget gives plenty of examples about how this magical thinking contributes to the child's explanation of time, space, and relationships with other people. These findings have been largely undisputed for more than half a century. But it doesn't take a world-renowned theorist to recognize that young children live in a world where things happen because people wish them to, and objects, animals, and nature all share thoughts and feelings. Any teacher who watches children make-believe knows this.

Make-believe play was part of what Piaget found most fascinating about children's development. Pretending represents their newfound ability to create and use symbols, humankind's most important achievement. This symbolic function is the basis for language development, but Piaget also studied how children's ability to construct mental images (or pictures in their heads) allows them to think about things that are not physically present. For example, a child hitches an imaginary horse to the front of a cardboard box, which she imagines is her enchanted carriage. She then "drives" to the ball (represented by making *clippety-clop* sounds). She is demonstrating a sophisticated ability to use sym-bols. She is literally *making* (herself and others) *believe* that these objects (horse, carriage, ball) and activities (hitching and driving) are present in the classroom.

This growing ability to represent (or *re*-present that which is not physically present) underpins not only oral language development but also reading and writing, the symbolic functions we prioritize in early childhood. As with all cog-nitive functions, each aspect of representation (speaking, listening, imagining, pretend play, drawing, writing, reading, and so on) takes time and practice to develop. When we expect young children to jump to use very abstract symbols in reading and writing without giving them the opportunity for many rich and extended experiences with less abstract forms of representation, we undermine their efforts.

This is one reason why many researchers encourage us to tell, as opposed to read, stories to children sometimes (Wineberg 2020). When we tell a story directly to children, the relationship with a caring person facilitates their engage-ment. Children make connections between the stories they hear and their exist-ing schema and experiences, visualizing their own mental images rather than viewing illustrations. What a powerful way to support emergent readers and writ-ers! With strong roots in oral language and clear-cut images, fairy tales are ideal for this. They are relatively easy for the teacher to learn to tell while their simple plots and familiar characters encourage children to imagine and reimagine them.

Representational ability is also a basis for a child's cognitive development and problem-solving ability. It coincides beautifully with the rich symbolic vocabulary shared by fairy tales, where the forest is the unknown; the castle is the place where quests begin and end; princesses and heroes become the quick embodiment of good, brave, and kind; and giants and witches represent the fearful and the bad. With this ready-made vocabulary of characters and themes, children can easily expand their own scenarios and imagery as they grow in their mastery of language, representation, play, and story.

Piaget and other theorists also help us understand why the violence in fairy tales we adults often find so troubling doesn't seem to bother even more sensitive children. In fairy tales, it is *not* the obedient and kindhearted Cinderella or the resourceful and well-intentioned Jack who are ultimately punished. Instead, the selfish, cruel, and dishonest characters face the consequences of their bad choices. According to Piaget (1965), children see the world of justice as black and white, where the good are always rewarded and the bad are punished, and the worse the behavior, the more drastic the punishment. With experience and cognitive development, children grow into a more nuanced understanding of right, wrong, and fairness. They begin to look at intention as a factor in whether an action is good or bad, rather than just the actual consequence. Once this happens, they find it easier to forgive a friend who accidentally knocks over their block tower than the bully who kicks it over on purpose.

Fairy Tales and Resilience

Additional characteristics of fairy tales can help explain their perennial popularity with children. In most cases, for example, the youngest child ends up being the hero. Rarely do the rich and powerful become the heroes. The young and seemingly disadvantaged characters are the ones who outwit the bad guys, witches, trolls, and dragons and go on to save the day. This speaks to the experiences of even the most privileged and secure children: What five-year-old has not felt weak and powerless in the world of big kids, adults, and the unknown?

This desire to rise above challenges is core to both fairy tales *and* resilience. Whether the challenge is to find one's brother who was snatched by the Snow Queen or to climb to the top of the playground slide for the first time, overcoming fears and bringing your strengths forward is what resilience is all about. While cultures around the world and through time have valued different strengths and faced different fears, resilience itself is universal (Masten 2015). Not surprisingly, most fairy tales capture the protective factors for resilience in a way that resonates with young children: in story form, wrapped in a magic cloak.

Fairy Tales and Vivian Paley's Storytelling/Storyacting

Early childhood educator Vivian Paley spent her career exploring children's relationship with stories. Through careful observations and reflections, Paley documented children's fluid travel between the stories they play, the stories they listen to, and the stories they write and act out (see, for example, Paley 1984, 1988, 1990, 1992, 1997, 2001, 2004, 2010). She recognized that by meeting children in the magical kingdom where they engage with story, educators' goals for literacy, social-emotional development, and classroom management could be woven together in the vibrant tapestry of the classroom community.

Like most early educators, Paley offered a wide range of children's literature to her preschoolers and kindergartners. However, she frequently chose to share folktales and fairy tales. She also told her classes stories of her own creation that were modeled after fairy tales. She used common fairy tale plot structures and stock characters like the Princess and the Witch for several reasons. Children readily responded to them, and the familiar characters and motifs translated smoothly into children's play. Paley also found that the simple and straightforward plots were a good match for children's developing storytelling and writing skills.

Paley was not immune to concerns about fairy tales discussed previously. She reflected on these issues often and discussed them with colleagues. Always sensitive to making her classroom a safe and inviting place for every child, Paley wanted to be sure the stories she shared were acceptable to all. After much debate, Paley concluded that the value of fairy tales to children's social and emotional development outweighed the challenges that their use in a classroom posed: "Putting aside the fact that fairy tales cannot be avoided, why are they needed? Perhaps because they are such good stories" (Paley 1990, 163).

To this end, Paley chose to tell the stories rather than read them. This allowed the children to give input along the way, therefore promoting their initiative. As active participants, the young listeners guided their teacher/storyteller to plot twists and resolutions that they could control and then reflect on. Often she found the children's own imaginings more frightening than the original stories she told. She gave the example of a child who had asked not to be told "Jack and the Beanstalk" as it was written. However, as the class discussed why the giant's wife had hidden Jack and wondered whether the giant's wife has a little boy of her own, the same child suggested that perhaps the giant had eaten his first child by mistake (Paley 1990). Paley reflected, "If given enough time, the children will take my questions, good and bad, to the same place: the fate of a vulnerable child surrounded by uncertainty and danger" (Paley 1990, 155). This fascination with the resilience of others seems to be at the heart of children's enjoyment of the stories.

Paley is best known for the storytelling/storyacting strategy she developed and refined. Paley saw storytelling/storyacting as the logical bridge between children's make-believe play and their emergent literacy skills. In her process, children dictate stories to a teacher or scribe who records exactly what they say. This allows children to take full control over their storymaking and promotes initiative and self-efficacy (and sometimes persistence, in the case of long stories or many interruptions!).

Then, at the end of every morning in Paley's classroom, children acted out their stories with their classmates, with the teacher serving as narrator. Paley believed this acting out of each story was especially important in developing a community of learners. Children shared and helped develop each other's ideas, just as they did in play, and brought these shared symbols into their later play and conversations with each other. In addition, seeing their own stories acted out encouraged children's reflection, growing an understanding of themselves as young readers and writers and promoting self-efficacy.

Discussed in more detail in chapter 3, research finds that storytelling/ storyacting is effective in promoting social-emotional skills related to resilience as well as literacy (Nicolopoulou et al. 2015). It likewise aligns with research on fairy tales and emotional regulation, supporting the idea that telling, retelling, and acting out fairy tales in a group setting is especially well-suited for children's development of self-regulation, a pivotal protective factor for resilience.

Fairy Tales and Emotional Regulation: Doubleness

Researchers Fleer and Hammer (2013) explore the relationship between fairy tales and self-regulation. They first identify two major challenges facing early childhood education: (1) the artificial split between cognitive and social-emotional development in early care and education because of the increased emphasis on early academics; and (2) the historic transfer of supporting young children's emotional regulation from families to teachers because of the increase in number of children who are in group care and education from an early age. Both challenges, they believe, can best be addressed by understanding how young children learn to recognize and identify physically felt emotions and to articulate feelings, which are the cognitive and cultural aspects of these emotions.

There are, of course, many ways teachers can approach the recognition, identification, and discussion of feelings in young children. But these researchers advocate for the inclusion of fairy tales as an intentional part of a curriculum that promotes emotional regulation. A group setting mirrors the way these stories were originally told; the storyteller and listeners gathered together as equal participants in the tale, which became a shared, communal experience (Martin 1999). In a classroom, a teacher and children can work together to promote emotional regulation as they explore fairy tales in both storytelling and play. With the teacher facilitating the exploration of fairy tales, children become more aware of the emotions that they, their peers, and the characters express.

Fleer and Hammer draw their rationale from another of the theoretical fairy godfathers of early childhood, Lev Vygotsky, and researchers who followed him. Consider what Vygotsky called the "doubleness" of children's emotional expression, which they experience in play and when listening to fairy tales. Doubleness is children's ability to simultaneously feel *happy* because they are playing with their friends but also *scared*, in the context of that play, because of the fire-breathing dragon outside their castle. Children have to regulate both emotions if the story is to move forward in play. If their delight in playing together isn't regulated, children dissolve into giggles and hugs. Conversely, if they can't regulate their fear of the "dragon," everyone will be crying and running for the door.

Fairy tales provide the ideal source of such doubleness. The stories offer the predictability and comfort of a magical world that children have come to know, as well as relationships that are easy to identify with. It is in part this predictability that makes fairy tales such a popular play theme. At the same time, fairy tales serve up fear of the villain or the daunting quest. This doubleness allows children to learn to identify and regulate their emotions.

Fairy Tales and Neuroscience: Transportation

Much of the evidence for the role that fairy tales can play in developing resilience relies on theoretical constructs rather than empirical research. However, recent advances in neuroscience may also support these ideas, including research by Berkeley's Greater Good Science Center at the University of California (Smith 2016). The researchers examined how we respond physiologically to stories, to better understand the instinct to tell stories and how stories may shape our thinking and behavior, and focused specifically on our stress response. As we discussed in chapter 1, stress in the human brain gets triggered by things other than physical threats. It is unlikely that we will ever encounter real dragons, or even wild animals like lions. However, characters *do* face them in stories. As Smith explains, "We're attracted to stressful stories because . . . we want to imagine how we would deal with all the many kinds of dragons that could rear up in our lives, from family strife, to layoffs, to crime" (Smith 2016, 2).

Neuroscientists discovered that hearing about conflict or threat in stories raises cortisol levels, which stimulates problem-solving responses. Similarly, characters in stories who garner our empathy stimulate the production of oxytocin, even though the characters are imaginary. This combination of cortisol (which produces attention/slight anxiety in the brain) and oxytocin (which produces the emotion of caring) results in the body responding to the story as though it were real, a phenomenon researchers call *transportation*. According to this research, when the story has a happy ending, the limbic system releases dopamine, the neurotransmitter that sends messages about pleasure. A sense of optimism and hope floods the body, as though the story is happening in real life (Smith 2016).

Smith focused his research on people's physiological responses to modern literature and media that draw inspiration from fairy tales, such as Star Wars and Harry Potter, rather than on traditional fairy tales themselves. The neurological processes at work as we listen to these archetypical stories trigger the parts of the brain involved in the development of resilience, as discussed in chapter 1. As such, his research offers another reason for teachers to embrace fairy tales as a way to explicitly align early childhood curriculum with the current model of resilience.

Fairy Tales and Cultural Affirmation

Folklorists, psychologists, and storytellers have long discussed the other reason that fairy tales resonate with children—and the rest of us—as we charge through the twenty-first century. Good stories get remembered and retold because they touch something meaningful in us. Because these stories have been handed down, reimagined, shared, changed, and retold again and again for centuries, they represent the significant distilled wisdom of the world's diverse cultural heritages. This is true today, when families annually view their favorite movies or read their favorite holiday book together. It was true in ancient times too, when the storytellers and sages worked hard to learn and tell aloud stories that would please their listeners. Only the robust stories that connected with people's challenges and emotions made it to the second telling.

Perhaps this is why some of our most beloved fairy tales, like "Cinderella" and "Beauty and the Beast," have been told for hundreds, if not thousands of years. Popular media in the United States and Europe have made the versions of these stories from England, Germany, and France more well-known than their cousins from Egypt, Japan, and Zimbabwe. However, the relationships, emotions, and challenges imagined in these diverse variants form a common thread that helps us recognize that at their core they are the same stories.

The fairy tales we read as picture books in our classrooms today have deep roots in cultures and people from whom we have much to learn. Their wisdom was passed down "in a symbolic, metaphoric story language and then honed by centuries of tongue-polishing to a crystalline perfection" as Yolen (1981, 18) writes in her book *Touch Magic: Fantasy, Faerie and Folklore in the Literature of Childhood*. It is this "tongue polished" affirmation of the universality of resilience that serves children as they navigate through twenty-first-century forests of challenges, both known and unknown.

Young children are surrounded by the symbols of the shared culture of traditional folklore: from Cinderella's glass slipper and Aladdin's magic lamp to the superheroes that draw from the pantheon of Greek gods for their inspiration. Like their predecessors who sat around fires and shared tales of wonder with spellbound audiences, modern writers and storytellers of folklore weave together threads of stories heard and imagined with their lived experiences, on a loom of their own cultural perspective.

In the twenty-first century, it is impossible to know the "original" version of any folktale. This is especially true when we consider those collected from Indigenous cultures by eager European and American folklorists who usually lacked both the language skills and cultural sensitivity to capture the nuances and deeper meanings in these tales. We do not know whether fairy tales from the oral tradition seem familiar because the people who recorded them tweaked them to be more like their own stories, or if they were swapped as cultures traded and dispersed as groups migrated, or whether, as some have suggested, they were independently imagined because our challenges and relationships are more the same than they are different.

As J. R. R. Tolkien, creator of *The Hobbit*, wrote, "It is now beyond all skill but that of the elves to unravel it" (Tolkien 1965, 20). Nonetheless, exploring the ancient tales of magic from which these familiar cultural symbols emerged connects our diverse and curious young learners with a complex web of Story that has always been about resilience. In the next chapters, we'll use all this research to create joyful, playful learning experiences for young children, tapping into the extraordinary magic of fairy tales to create the ordinary magic of resilience.

Discover More

Vivian Gussin Paley has written thirteen books in which she shares deep insights on children's play, storytelling, relationships, and emergent literacy. Current favorites include *The Girl with the Brown Crayon* (1997) and *You Can't Say You Can't Play* (1992).

No time for a book? For ideas on how Paley uses story to address every aspect of her curriculum, including classroom management, read her interview in *Young Children* (Dombrink-Green 2011).

Jane Yolen has written over four hundred books as of 2021, including many inspired by fairy tales, and she's still writing! Her *Touch Magic* (originally published in 1981 and revised in 2005) is a thoughtful collection of short essays on how important fairy tales are to children.

Need to brush up on all those theories? *Theories of Early Childhood Education* (Cohen and Waite-Stupiansky 2017) is an accessible and comprehensive look at the people who influenced developmentally appropriate practice.

Waving The Magic Wand of Resilience:
How This Book Is Organized

The first two chapters of this book discuss *why* using fairy tales in an early childhood classroom supports resilience and literacy in all children, and why this is especially important for children who have experienced trauma and toxic stress. The rest of the book is about *how* to do this. This chapter describes how to navigate the chapters that focus on individual fairy tales.

Each fairy tale chapter has the following sections:

1. **Story Magic**
   Each chapter begins with information about the fairy tale and its variants, and how the story connects with the protective factors of resilience, and offers suggestions for your story center and storytelling/storyacting.

2. **Caring Magic**
   This section offers suggestions for activities related to the story that help children make connections with each other and the significant adults in their lives.

3. **Doing Magic**

   Divided into two parts, Playing Magic and Making Magic, this section
   has suggestions for adapting your classroom learning centers to support
   children's engagement with the fairy tale as they develop resilience, along
   with specific projects that promote initiative and executive functions.

4. **Superpower Magic**

   Activities, songs, or games related to the story that foster self-regulation
   are included in this section, as well as ways the story can be used to support calm, integrated transitions and routines.

Additional information about how to use the Story Magic, Caring Magic, Doing
Magic, and Superpower Magic sections is found below.

Story Magic

Each story section starts off with a description of a fairy tale or folktale. The plot
is summarized, with interesting tidbits about the history of the story.

Versions and Variants to Consider

Because there are so many great variants of each story, the book provides just
a handful of titles from different cultures to get you started. Seek these books
and more at your local public library. Dedicated children's librarians have more
folktale and fairy tale recommendations than a magic harp has songs, and they
are eager to share them with you! Garage sales, thrift stores, and used bookstores
(in your local community or online) are great sources, and new versions are being
published all the time.

Children love to hear the same story over and over again, and with each repetition, their understanding of the story and its language, structure, and imagery
deepens. Many child development experts believe that young children actually
need to hear the same story over and over. Why else would so many children
demand the same story at bedtime for weeks? This effect is compounded when
variants of the same story from different cultures or authors are shared together.
Younger children express excitement when they discover similarities and differences in setting, characters, or plot twists. Older children can analyze these
differences in more explicit compare-and-contrast activities.

It is especially effective when you ask children from different cultural or
linguistic traditions (or their families) to select a variant of a familiar tale from
their home cultures. This makes them feel welcomed and lets all children hear

and relate to the stories their friends enjoy at home. You may also want to consult friends or colleagues familiar with these cultures or do an online search if you are not sure whether a book you have chosen from a given culture includes hurtful stereotypes or biases. (See appendix B for more on this.) You can invite family members to share folktales orally or read stories that represent resilience to them. You can also retell familiar tales and include characters with diverse abilities or nonnuclear family structures. All of these strategies highlight the universality of resilience and ensure that you are using fairy tales to promote both resilience and equity in your classroom.

Themes of Resilience

After each story is described, there is a brief description of how the protective factors of resilience (attachment and relationships, initiative and executive functions, and self-regulation) come out in the story. These are provided to get you thinking about the "ordinary magic" of resilience and are certainly not exhaustive. Once you start looking for resilience, you'll see it everywhere.

Questions to Explore the Protective Factors for Resilience

Suggestions for open-ended questions to get children thinking about each protective factor follow. These may be used while you're reading, if you use a dialogic reading approach, at the end of the reading, or as the children connect to the story in their play.

Like all open-ended questions, they do not have right or wrong answers but rather deepen children's thinking and uncover their unique perspectives. Because children's experiences, thinking, and language development vary so greatly, you may decide the questions are too challenging or not challenging enough. Use them to inspire other open-ended questions to ponder with children as you share the story.

Additions to the Story Center

A well-equipped and engaging story center (often called a writing center) is an easy way to encourage preschoolers to write. Story centers are the cheapest and easiest of the centers to establish, yet in many early childhood classrooms they are used only for alphabet practice, if they are present at all. Crayons, markers, pencils, and paper are all it takes—add mini-staplers and you have your own publishing house. The story center section for each fairy tale includes suggestions of items related to the story that you may add to your center to encourage the children to draw, tell, and write about the connections they are making.

Ideas for Storytelling/Storyacting

As we discussed in the previous chapter, Vivian Paley's storytelling/storyacting process is a powerful way to build resilience and literacy at the same time. Each Story Magic section includes a few ideas specific to the fairy tale that you may watch for as children act out their stories. The suggestions are made to support enjoyment of the storytelling/storyacting process as you extend the children's learning, which may or may not be relevant to your class. For example, after reading "Rapunzel" for a week, none of your students may even mention a tower in their stories! This is a good indication that that it is not an image or idea they want to explore now. You can find detailed suggestions for bringing the storytelling/storyacting process into your class at the end of this chapter (see page 33).

Ordinary Magic throughout the Curriculum

For children to explore the stories and the themes of resilience deeply, they need to be active and play. As much as we value oral language development, we know talking is never enough for young children! Each Story Magic section, therefore, is followed by suggestions for classroom materials, projects, activities, and games that support children's integration of the meaning of the story.

Many of these align with literacy, art, and STEM standards. However, they are presented in the context of the protective factors for resilience: attachment/relationships (Caring Magic), initiative/executive functions (Doing Magic), and self-regulation (Superpower Magic). These divisions are somewhat artificial, and most developmentally appropriate and playful learning opportunities support development of all of these protective factors. But by focusing on each one individually and specifically describing how the activities promote the protective factors, we hope you will be inspired to adapt your own favorite experiences for children to support resilience more intentionally. Needless to say, just as you should pre-read each book you share with children, it's always best to try out activities in advance!

There are also suggestions that teachers, therapists, and other professionals working with children with additional support needs may find useful. In this way, a child's support from all the magical helpers works even more effectively.

Caring Magic—the Protective Factor of Relationships

Caring Magic suggestions offer opportunities for all children to develop relationships with each other, as well as with the adults in the classroom. Some activities focus on helping children collaborate with multiple peers so that they can develop skills in communicating their own ideas and respecting differences. Others focus on perspective taking, a cognitive skill that involves being able to understand that we each see things from very different points of view, a challenge for young children. Still others focus on seeing oneself as a vital part of a group. All develop the social and emotional skills necessary to make and keep friends in play situations and to respond positively to the caring adults in one's life.

Doing Magic—the Protective Factor of Initiative and Executive Functions

Doing Magic is divided into two sections: Playing Magic and Making Magic. The focus is supporting children to act on their ideas, persist in solving problems, and feel a sense of agency—the awareness that they have some positive control.

Playing Magic is a list of story-related items to add to common learning centers in a classroom to spark children's connection to the fairy tale. Ideas may be suggested for the following centers:

1. Dramatic play center

2. Blocks/building center

3. Art center

4. Outdoor play area

5. Sand/water/sensory areas

6. Discovery/science center

7. Math/manipulative center

The lists are starting places to inspire your own, and the children's, ideas. Most are accessible and easy to collect. Specific commercial products are not listed. Open-ended and flexible materials that invite imaginative play are more conducive to the development of initiative and executive function skills. A complete list of common materials is found in appendix A.

Making Magic suggests more specific activities that involve children in tinkering, creating, and making, based on the imagery from the story. Most involve a teacher's facilitation and are more in-depth. However, the focus continues to be on children's active construction of knowledge and their problem-finding and problem-solving skills.

Superpower Magic—the Protective Factor of Self-Regulation

Self-regulation truly *is* a superpower for young children. We ask them to float invisibly down hallways so they don't bother other classes. They are expected to magically produce words to describe the swirl of feelings bubbling around their internal cauldrons. And when they want to be the first to play with the new dragon toy, they have to freeze like ice and wait their turn.

This section includes games, activities, and transition cues that support children's self-regulation skills, including focused attention, controlled movement, shifting perspective, deep breathing, feeling identification, and emotional regulation. Many involve creative movement and most engage the child's imagination and engagement with story to scaffold their regulatory processes.

A Few More Lanterns to Light Your Way

In addition to the six fairy tale chapters that follow, the appendices offer helpful information and resources as you begin your exploration of the tales. Appendix A, Materials for Classroom Magic, contains lists of common loose parts and found items that can enhance not only children's investigations of these stories but other topics as well. Appendix B, Fairy Tale Variants, includes a list of the variants listed in the chapters, as well as useful information about how to choose stories to share with young children with an eye to equity and cultural sensitivity. Appendix C shares some of the myriad children's books that also feature themes of resilience, as well as additional practical and accessible resources about trauma and teaching for resilience throughout your curriculum. Finally, a seventh bonus fairy tale chapter, "Beauty and the Beast: The Magic of Being True to Yourself," can be found online.

www.redleafpress.org
/her/bab.pdf

There are thousands of folktales and fairy tales from around the world, and most of them exemplify resilience. Fairy tale heroes shine with this ability to bounce back from adversity—whether it be a dragon, a wicked stepmother, or a tall mountain they must climb—to get to the happily-ever-after. Likewise, there are more wonderful and magical ways children can connect with stories than there are sparkles on Cinderella's gown! The fairy tale chapters that follow are invitations for you to start exploring this vast domain of literature as you nurture the developing brain in *every* child, giving them the best chance of living happily ever resiliently!

How to Use Vivian Paley's Storytelling/Storyacting Process

1. Set up a story table with paper, crayons, and so on. This can be your story center; a smaller, more private space; or even a clipboard that a scribe brings to a corner of the carpet area.

2. Identify a scribe who will write down children's stories. This can be a teacher, an assistant, a family member, a volunteer, or even an older student (usually middle school or above works best).

3. Announce to the group that the storytelling/storyacting center is open, and invite children to tell their stories.

4. Have the scribe write down exactly what the child says. It's fine to ask clarifying questions, but the goal is to have children's own stories recorded. They may be very short at first; this is expected.

5. After the story is completed, the scribe may underline each character. Characters can be trees, fences, rainbows, or anything, as young children add human characteristics to inanimate objects. Underlining the characters will make the storyacting time go more smoothly.

6. Stories should be acted out the same day they are dictated—at circle time, before lunch, after rest time, or whenever it can be consistently added to the daily schedule.

7. At the designated time, gather all children in the "story circle." Consider using masking tape to make a large square "stage" within the circle, as it provides the actors boundaries and helps add to the event's special feeling.

8. The author of the story chooses which character they would like to be. The teacher then identifies other children to play the rest of the roles. These children come up to the stage. Note: Paley found it most effective to go around the circle and invite each child to participate until all roles are filled so everyone gets the chance to act.

9. The teacher cues the children to get ready for the storyplay. In my classroom, I said, "3, 2, 1, storyplay begins, ACTION!" Whatever the cues are, they should be consistent each time. The expectations for children's behavior should be clear: actors only in the stage area, while the audience watches; all voices silent once the final word of the cue is said. (This helps build self-regulation, and most children are eager to see the story, so they willingly comply!)

10. The teacher reads the story as the children act it out. Beginning actors might need a few suggestions ("Can you be a cat? Show me how a cat might move"). Generally after children become used to the process, they come up with their own interpretations of the characters, which promotes initiative.

11. At the conclusion of the story, the teacher says, "The end," or some other cue that this story is over. You may wish to repeat the title of the story and the author's name. I always invite children to clap, although this is not necessary.

12. The actors and author return to their seats. The next author is called up, and the process repeats.

Trisha Lee (2016), who shares storytelling/storyacting in the United Kingdom, suggests introducing the process for the first time by bringing a story from a previous group.

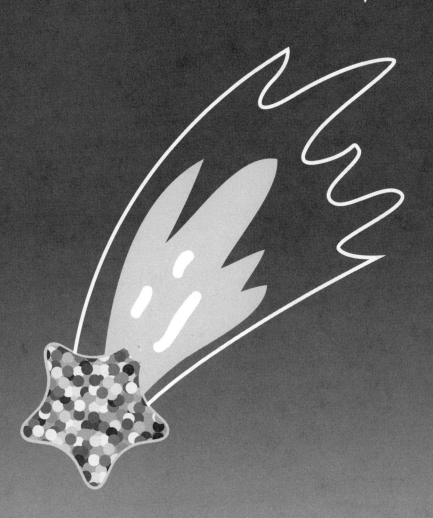

Part Two:
Fairy Tale Magic
in the
Classroom

Cinderella: The Magic of Resilience around the World

Story Magic

A father is widowed and left with a young daughter. He marries another woman who has her own daughter(s). Soon after the wedding, the woman shows her true nature. Believing her stepdaughter's kind heart and lovely face make her own daughters look bad, the stepmother dresses her in rags and has her do all the work in the house. This the girl does without complaining. When an invitation comes for a ball where the prince will choose his bride, the woman and her daughters don't allow the girl to come. After they leave, the girl cries, and a magical being (usually a fairy godmother) appears. She transforms the girl's rags into a lovely gown, with sparkling shoes to match, and tells her that she must leave the ball by midnight. The girl goes to the ball, and everyone is amazed by her beauty, including the prince, who spends the evening dancing with her. She leaves in time and is waiting in rags by the time her stepmother and stepsisters return. The same thing happens the following evening (in many variants), but this time the heroine is so happy with the prince that she forgets to watch the clock. Just in time, she runs from the palace, but in her haste, she loses one of her shoes. The prince finds the shoe and declares that he will marry the owner. All the maidens in the land try on the shoe, but it fits no one. Finally, the heroine asks to try, over the loud protests of her stepmother and stepsisters. The shoe fits perfectly, and she and the prince are married and live happily ever after.

Versions and Variants to Consider

"Cinderella" is such a familiar story! In addition to many movies, books, and cartoons, the symbols of the fairy godmother and the glass slipper can be found in advertising, popular media, music, and just about everywhere. The story has been told all over the world for centuries. Many versions are far older than the one written down by Charles Perrault in the 1600s, which Disney used as the basis for its famous film. The variants listed below, with a focus on picture book versions from a variety of cultural traditions, are just the tip of the magic wand. Most children's librarians know lots more options to help you find ones that will work best with your group of children. "Cinderella" is a wonderful way to explore how story brings together children's many home cultures.

Cinderella, written and illustrated by Marcia Brown, is still found in most libraries because Brown won the Caldecott Medal for the delicately painted line drawings in 1955. The plot will be familiar to children who have seen the Disney movie.

Cinderella, retold by Amy Ehrlich and illustrated by Susan Jeffers, features lovely, large illustrations with lots of detail.

Yeh Shen, retold by Ai-Ling Louie and illustrated by Ed Young, is a Chinese version of Cinderella. A magical talking fish is the only friend of the heroine, Yeh Shen. After the stepmother kills the fish for dinner, a mysterious old man tells Yeh Shen to bury the fish's bones and to ask them for help when she needs it. The fish's bones transform Yeh Shen's ragged clothes into a beautiful gown and give her golden slippers so she can attend a feast and meet her future husband.

Chinye: A West African Folk Tale, written by Obi Onyefulu and illustrated by Evie Safarewicz, transfers many of the motifs of "Cinderella" to a story told by the Igbo people in Nigeria. Instead of being rewarded by marrying a prince, the heroine receives riches for being brave, kind, and obedient and shares them with her village so that everyone prospers.

The Golden Sandal, retold by Rebecca Hickock and illustrated by Will Hillenbrand, is from Iraq. Although neither the author nor the illustrator are Iraqi, both the story and pictures are well researched and authentic for the time period. The

facial expressions in the illustrations are great starting points to discuss what the characters might be feeling. Like the Chinese Yeh Shen, Maha, the heroine, has a magical fish who helps transform her life after she spares his.

The Gift of the Crocodile, retold by Judy Sierra and illustrated by Reynold Ruffins, comes from the Moluccas in Indonesia. The daughter herself persuades her father to marry the neighboring widow, only to discover her stepmother's true nature after the wedding. A crocodile she befriends while washing clothes in the river is the magical "fairy godmother" in this story.

The Rough-Face Girl, written by Rafe Martin and illustrated by David Shannon, is inspired by a Mi'kmaq tale with themes similar to "Cinderella." Mistreated by her sisters, the youngest sister has singed hair and burns on her face from working over the fire. While all the young women in the village try to win the hand of the Invisible Being, the youngest sister succeeds not by dressing up with magic but rather by seeing him with her pure heart.

Little Gold Star/Estrellita de oro: A Cinderella Cuento, retold by Joe Hayes and illustrated by Gloria Osuna Perez and Lucia Angela Perez, is a Spanish American Cinderella tale, written in both English and Spanish. The heroine is rewarded for being kind and hardworking by the appearance of a gold star on her forehead. But when her stepsisters try for the same prize, they find a donkey ear and a cow horn growing out of their heads—not exactly appealing to the prince!

The Irish Cinderlad, retold by Shirley Climo and illustrated by Loretta Krupinski, features a plucky young Irish boy with giant feet as the hero. Cinderlad must conquer a giant and dragon with help from a magical bull "fairy godmother."

Ashpet, retold by Joanne Compton and illustrated by Kenn Compton, is an Appalachian version of the story. Along with many other folktales that settlers brought over from European countries, it changed to match the new landscapes and culture. Ashpet's kindness wins the heart of an old neighbor lady who magics her a lovely red gingham dress with matching shoes to wear to the picnic. Rather than losing her shoe, she tosses it into the bushes and asks the doctor's son (kind of a prince!) to find it as a distraction so she can run home on time.

Glass Slipper, Gold Sandal: A Worldwide Cinderella, written by Paul Fleishman and illustrated by Julie Paschkis, is a seamless retelling that combines Cinderella stories from countries all over the world into one story.

Themes of Attachment and Relationships

While it's easy to think of this as a story about the relationship between the hardworking heroine and her prince, or even her wicked stepmother, two other relationships lie at the heart of most "Cinderella" variants: the sibling rivalry and the relationship between Cinderella and a magical helper. These relationships are pivotal to resilience and also within most children's experience.

Sibling rivalry occurs in even the happiest families. If a sibling has something a child wants, whether it is a new toy, a trip to the store with Dad, or the chance to pick the TV show, rivalry or jealousy can bubble up. These feelings may be exacerbated when the sibling is a new baby or when one child gets more attention because their needs are different. Child development experts like Dr. T. Berry Brazelton (Brazelton and Sparrow 2005) tell us that sibling rivalry is the perfect context for children to understand differences in perspective and learn social problem-solving skills, but families and teachers often have a hard time appreciating this when petty rivalries threaten the peace! Talking with children about these feelings can also be a challenge. We all know that you're supposed to love and be kind to your siblings. Negative feelings are difficult to identify as normal and natural, so we tend to admonish children for having them rather than labeling them and helping the child deal with the feelings appropriately. That's why this classic example of sibling rivalry is so powerful for children. We have *all* felt like Cinderella! The story shows them that children are not alone, and with persistence and patience, things can turn out well.

And why do things turn around for Cinderella? She turns to a competent adult for help. Young children may not have a fairy godmother or a talking fish, but they have grandparents, teachers, neighbors, and others. Recognizing that trusted adults are on their side is a valuable resilience lesson, and this is especially true for children whose family situation is insecure.

Note: In some variants, Cinderella invites her stepsisters to live in the palace with her and the prince; in others, the sisters have their eyes pecked out by birds. As you share the stories, remember that young children usually are more satisfied when mean people are punished and good people are rewarded. This is developmentally appropriate. Be open to children's responses to the different endings and recognize that that it's okay if they don't embrace the kinder, gentler treatment of the bad guys just yet!

Questions to Explore the Protective Factor of Attachment with Children

1. How do you think Cinderella felt when her sisters went to the ball and she couldn't? Have you ever had something like that happen to you? How did you feel? What did you do to feel better?

2. When Cinderella felt sad, her fairy godmother appeared (or she went to talk to the fish, depending on the version). Can you think of a time when you were sad and went to someone to help you? How did they help you feel better?

Themes of Initiative

The protective factor of initiative might feel absent in "Cinderella," at least in the most familiar variant in the United States based on the Disney movie. The heroine passively accepts her family's bullying and only gets to go to the ball because a magical being helps her. But many other Cinderellas take more control of their situations. The Spanish American "Little Gold Star" asks her father to shear her sheep so she can spin the wool and weave him a blanket. While she washes it, a hawk appears and gives her the gold star. Ashpet, from Appalachia, hides her shoe in the bushes and asks the prince/doctor's son to hunt for it so she can get home on time.

But let's look at where we do find initiative in all the versions: Cinderella's hard work. Young children take much pride in doing real work—this is why "helper" is such a coveted job! Think of a child's joy when they get to wield a broom or move tables and chairs. This demonstrates self-efficacy: *I can do it!* Even in Marcia Brown's more traditional retelling, Cinderella is asked to help dress her sisters for the ball, not just to be mean, but because of her skill: "They called in Cinderella to ask her advice, for she had very good taste in these matters."

In addition, both children's and the Cinderellas' tasks involve the executive function of working memory. For example, understanding the sequence of washing the dishes and performing it consistently requires working memory. Just imagine the amount of focus it would take to separate lentils from a pile of rice, as some heroines must do to go to the ball!

Questions to Explore the Protective Factor of Initiative with Children

1. What are some jobs that Cinderella did in the story? Which do you think you could do?

2. What jobs do you like to do to help your family or in our classroom? How do you feel when you do them?

3. What is the hardest job you've ever helped with?

Themes of Self-Regulation

Most versions of the Cinderella story require the heroine to exhibit great self-regulation. When she finally gets to the ball, festival, or picnic, she has a marvelous time. And yet she *must* leave by the stroke of midnight. As hard as that is, she does so—sometimes just in the nick of time. Even those of us with well-developed self-regulation skills would be challenged by this! In most variants, Cinderella does not know what will happen if she doesn't leave on time, but she follows the directions anyway. What a great model of self-regulation for children who know what it's like to have so much fun playing that they lose track of time and don't want to stop!

Questions to Explore the Protective Factor of Self-Regulation with Children

1. Why do you think Cinderella left the ball so quickly that she lost her shoe?

2. Tell me about a time that you were having so much fun doing something that you didn't want to stop. What did you do?

Additions to the Story Center

Like many fairy tales, Cinderella sparkles with magic and transformation. You can make your story center sparkle too!

- Add glitter pens, pencils, markers, or crayons. Bringing them out only during specific stories or units adds to the magic and extends how long they last.

- Tie ribbons to the ends of regular writing tools.

- Place writing tools in inexpensive plastic containers that mimic glass or crystal.

- Glue plastic "gems" to the outside of a plastic cup or box, or put some in the bottom so that markers or scissors stand up.

- Offer fancy paper to inspire young storytellers. Dollar stores often have discounted paper with lacy or colorful designs; cut in half or quarters.

- Stick "jewels" onto small staplers to get children excited to make their own books.

- Add "fairy lights" to draw children into the story center. Drape the lights along the wall or stuff a short string of battery-operated lights inside a cut-off two-liter bottle.

Ideas for Storytelling/Storyacting

It is hard to know which images will pop up most in children's Cinderella-inspired stories. Expect a focus on princesses, talking mice, and fairy godmothers if they have seen the Disney movie. If you have shared several cultural variants, children will more likely focus on the central themes of the story: sibling rivalry, the stroke of midnight, and a magical helper.

If children mention a clock or time, consider making the clock a character. The children will be playing a clock game in the self-regulation section on page 51, and a clock character can be encouraged to use their arms like clock hands and make ticking and bonging noises.

If a story incorporates the magical helper, ask them how they will show their magic: How will they pretend to have a wand or otherwise twinkle around the main character so they know they are transformed? You can prompt the transformed character to imagine changing from rags into fancy clothes (or from a cat to a lion, or any other transformation the children imagine). Can they show how that feels? The focus should be on allowing the children to translate the images in their heads into bodily movements.

The traditional Cinderella stories have many female characters; watch if children change the gender of the siblings and the magical helpers they include in the story. It's important to give all children the chance to participate in story-telling/storyacting. If gender roles are limiting, go around the circle and choose children for roles in the order they are seated. Preschoolers may giggle at a boy playing a stepsister or a girl playing the prince, but they soon get caught up in the spirit of the story. This, in turn, supports their developing understanding of gender equity and the importance of all positive character traits, regardless of who is displaying them.

Caring Magic
Cinderella Helper Coupon

While we all feel sorry for Cinderella getting stuck with all the housework, children actually love to help and do grown-up chores! In this activity, they get to pick jobs that help parents, caregivers, siblings, or friends.

You will need:

- Note cards or paper cut to desired size
- Catalogs and magazines
- Glue or tape
- Crayons or markers
- Colored tape or stickers (optional)

1. Discuss the jobs Cinderella did for her family. Ask what children like to do to help their families, brothers and sisters, teachers, or friends (choose just one or two categories for younger children). How do they feel when they help?

2. Have children look through magazines or catalogs to find pictures that remind them of jobs they can do to help someone. This may be a picture of a toy broom and dust pan, a box of diapers to bring to a baby, books they could put away, a jacket they help a friend zip, and so on.

3. When they find a picture, remove the page from the catalog so they can cut it out and glue or tape it to a note card.

4. On the back of the note card, ask the child to dictate to you how they help and then encourage them to decorate it if desired. (Note: Colored tape can "frame" immature cutting and cover up rough edges.)

5. Encourage children to take home the note card or put it in the cubby of a friend to show that person how they will help them.

How it builds attachment and relationships

Often children don't have the opportunity to show people they care through concrete actions. Thinking about how they can help builds self-confidence while letting them reflect on everyone's important role in a family, classroom, or friendship. If you know a child has a challenging home situation and the adults might not welcome these offers to help, suggest that they think of ways to help their classroom friends or their teachers. Note: Giving families the heads-up that this helper coupon is coming home as part of the Cinderella unit will help them appreciate their child's intention (and know what the card is for).

Classroom Ball

Almost every version of "Cinderella" includes a ball or festival. And what is a ball but a chance to come together and celebrate relationships! A ball can be at any time of the day, and all you really need is space for the children to move freely to music.

You will need:

- Guests: You can include just the children in your class. Or, if you choose to have it during the late afternoon when you have fewer children, consider inviting children from another classroom. Note: While involving families seems like a good idea, any event held during the day leaves out working parents. Consider more inclusive practices such as filming parts of the festivities or using technology like video chats to allow families to participate remotely.

- Music: Any kind of music will work, but consider classical music and not just because it's often played at balls. Often children are not used to hearing classical music, so they don't have preconceptions about how to move to it and may move more imaginatively and more slowly. You may need to model dancing to get them started, but most young children respond well to the music's interesting complexity. If you don't know what to pick, search video sites for classical music for children. The Cinderella Suite by Prokofiev, the soundtrack from *Fantasia*, or instrumental versions of Disney songs are all perfect.

- Optional materials to make it magical: Pieces of fabric to use as capes or gowns, construction paper crowns, tiaras, and swords made before or during the event, fairy lights, battery-operated candles, and food if desired.

Keep your ball simple, playful, and child centered. This is not a prom or major life celebration. It is an opportunity for children to pretend to be part of stories they have read and play with their friends in a new way. Child-made costumes better promote imagination and collaboration than prepackaged or teacher-made princess decorations.

How it builds attachment and relationships

When we interact with children in unique ways, they have a chance to see us in a new light, and we may see aspects of their personalities that we don't notice when we are slinging snacks, zipping coats, and wiping noses. Turning down the lights and putting on classical music to turn circle time into a magical ballroom lets their world sparkle with surprises and new possibilities. When we dance and wave scarves up and down as they do, we are showing them we respect their love of play and fantasy. We are all co-creators of a wonderful story.

This is why it's especially important to keep things calm and simple, despite our best intentions to make it a real "ball." Children are sensitive to our moods and stress, and children who have experienced trauma are hypervigilant. They will not enjoy this celebration if they pick up that you are tense and irritated because the decorations you spent three hours making don't fit on the wall without taking down the family notice board.

Doing Magic: Playing Magic
Props for Dramatic Play

- Aprons
- Child-sized broom, dustpan, feather duster, clean rags
- Shoes, shoes, and shoes (include very small shoes and slippers, and remember that several "Cinderella" variants have sandals)
- Fabric pieces and remnants to make capes, skirts, ball gowns, and other fancy wear (ask families if they have old scarves or leftover fabric from sewing projects)
- Plastic straws, construction paper, tape, ribbon, or yarn to make magic wands, crowns, swords, and so forth (keep in the art center if preferred)
- Stuffed animals or puppets of creatures from the stories (for example, mice, birds, lizards, and fish)

Props for Blocks/Building and STEM

- Books with pictures of castles or book(s) you make yourself using pictures found online that are laminated and then placed in a binder or attached with a ring
- Cardboard tubes (toilet paper, paper towels, and so on)
- Clear and colored transparent blocks or panels (these can be purchased or made by taping cellophane to cardboard frames)
- Variety of farm animals, including horses
- Wagons of various types
- People

Props for Sensory Tables

- Water table: Toy dishes and cookware, sponges, dish towels, plastic fish if you read "Cinderella" variants with the magic fish helper
- Sensory bins: In several versions, Cinderella has to sort lentils or grains of rice. Adapt this by adding small non-food items like pebbles, gems, or beads to your sand table, along with tweezers and containers where children can place the "lentils" they've picked out.
- Fairy dust sensory bins for individual play:
  - Line pan, tray, or box with gold or silver paper.
  - Fill a reclosable plastic bag with white play sand or table salt and add a few drops of liquid food coloring. Children can help mush the color into the sand in the bag—a great fine-motor activity!
  - Pour sand or salt into lined box.
  - Add glitter (biodegradable if possible) if desired.
  - Hide small jewels in the tray for children to find.
  - Provide a pencil wrapped in foil for children to draw in the fairy dust to reveal the shiny base.

Props for the Manipulative/Fine-Motor Center

- Lacing cards or boards
- Buttoning boards
- Beads and strings

Note: This unit may inspire children to rediscover these common early childhood materials because they are all things Cinderella did to help her sisters get ready for the ball.

Doing Magic: Making Magic
Shoe Prints

While some variants of this fairy tale do not mention Cinderella's famous shoes, many do, whether they are glass pumps, golden sandals, embroidered slippers, or even cowboy boots! This activity invites children to connect the story imagery with what is often a beloved possession and see ordinary shoes in a whole new light.

You will need:

- Large papers (either individual or mural sized)
- Tempera paint of various colors
- Pie tins for paint
- Paper towels to line pie tins
- A variety of old shoes that can get paint on them, such as baby shoes, children's shoes with different treads, doll shoes, flip-flops, and so on
- Paint smocks
- Table covering

1. Demonstrate to children how to make prints:

    ○ Press a shoe carefully down into paint in a pie pan (a layer of paper towels in the bottom will help make paint more like a rubber stamp pad).

    ○ Wipe off excess paint on the side of the pan.

    ○ Press the shoe onto the paper. (Younger children may drag the shoes rather than stamp them.)

2. Encourage children to make their own shoe prints. The colors will stay purer if you put one shoe in each pan or give each child a shoe and let them try it in one color of their choice.

3. Ask the children who the shoes might belong to or where they are going— is there a story to tell?

How it builds initiative and executive functions

Through this activity children develop two executive functions: cognitive flexibility and working memory. They are used to thinking of shoes as having one function: to wear on their feet! Seeing shoes as tools for making art and seeing the finished product encourages them to stretch their imaginations and view shoes in a different way. Shape, the imprint of the sole, and size become the shoes' most important characteristics, rather than their color or whether they are sandals or sneakers.

Working memory is activated as children remember the specific sequence of steps in this project. Children need to sublimate natural distractions like giggling about painting with shoes and telling stories as they focus on remembering the process steps.

Magic Color Calm-Down Jars

Just as Cinderella's fairy godmother magically transforms her rags into silk, this calm-down jar captures the magic of transformation as children use them to relax and practice self-regulation.

You will need:

- Plastic bottle or jar with lid for each child (jars with wider mouths make it easier for children to pour)
- Measuring cups (lightweight cups with defined spouts are easier to use)
- Water
- Baby oil
- Water-based food coloring
- Oil-based food coloring (if available)
- Large-sized glitter or sequins
- Toothpicks for stirring
- Glue for attaching lids (optional)

1. With children's help, measure enough water in a measuring cup to fill about half the jar. Demonstrate how to hold the jar with one hand and carefully pour the water in with the other. Then ask the children to do it.

2. Have children put two or three drops of water-based food coloring into the jar. Chant, "Drop, drop, not a lot," to develop the executive function of "effortful control," or self-regulation. Note: Because the color in the water will blend with the color in the oil, you may want to provide only primary colors.

3. Help the children tighten the lid and then have them shake jar to color the water.

4. Help children pour the same amount of oil as the water into a second measuring cup.

5. Assist children as they add a few drops of a different color of oil-based food coloring (the kind used for making candy, not gel colors).

6. Have children gently mix the food coloring into the oil with a toothpick.

7. Reopen the jar, and help the children pour in the oil mixture.

8. Ask the children to describe what they see (the oil sits on top of the water).

9. Allow children to carefully add sequins or glitter, help them to replace the lid, and then they can shake the jar again. (Add glue around the rim if you know children will shake too enthusiastically.)

10. Encourage the children to chant or sing "Pretty colors I can see / Now I shake it, magically!" to the tune of "Twinkle, Twinkle, Little Star."

11. While children will be excited by the mixing of the colors, encourage them to stop and hold the jar still to see what happens next. They may close their eyes during the transformation if they like.

How it builds initiative and executive functions

Calm-down jars or sensory jars are known for helping children with self-regulation challenges. This project encourages self-regulation as well as initiative. Children will try to figure out what happens to the colors (problem solving). By helping construct the jars, they are building independence and self-confidence. When a child has control of the jar because they've created it, they are more likely to use it to transform themselves from upset and anxious to calm and focused. The jars can be part of a child's self-initiated self-regulation routine, an additional way to promote self-efficacy.

Superpower Magic
Countdown to Midnight

This simple game works well when children are waiting in line or for circle time to start. No materials are needed.

1. Talk about what happens when Cinderella realizes it's almost midnight. Ask the children to stand and become big clocks by putting their feet slightly apart with their arms either down to their sides or, if there's room, at angles like a clock's hands.

2. Demonstrate "ticking" by rocking from foot to foot, saying, "Tick, tock, tick, tock," slowly and rhythmically.

3. After children are in a rhythm with rocking from foot to foot, tell them the clock is going to strike midnight when you say, "Bong, bong, bong," twelve times.

4. Ask the children to listen for the clock striking and run in place as fast as they can, just like Cinderella.

5. Have the children "hide" (stop running and cover their heads with their arms) as soon as the bonging stops. If you are transitioning to a sit-down activity, ask them to sit down and "hide."

6. Repeat as desired. Children can also lead the activity for their friends. Vary the number of "bongs" to increase or decrease the challenge.

How it builds self-regulation

Part of self-regulation is shifting from slow to fast and back again. Another aspect is coordinating two actions at once—listening for the "bong, bong, bong" to start while rocking back and forth saying, "Tick tock." Similarly, when children are running as fast as they can, they have to listen for the cue to stop and hide. Young children find this dual focus difficult, and like many familiar children's games, this offers a playful way to develop the skill.

Playdough Feelings

In this activity, children make snakes and balls from playdough while learning to identify emotions.

You will need:

- Playdough for every child
- Images from book versions of Cinderella (marked with sticky notes) that clearly show facial expressions of various characters

- A piece of paper or play mat with a circle drawn on it or a round paper plate for each child
- Small mirrors (optional)

1. Ask the children to roll a variety of snakes and balls to explore the playdough before the activity starts. Have them put their snakes and balls at the top of their paper.

2. Show the children a picture from one of the "Cinderella" variants you read. See if they can remember what is happening and guess what the characters are feeling based on their facial expressions.

3. Have children see if they can make the same faces, looking in the mirrors if available.

4. Ask the children to use their playdough snakes and balls (and other shapes, if desired) to create a face on their paper, play mat, or plate. Comment by identifying the feeling by saying, for example, "Oooh . . . she looks jealous!" "Wow, that is a mad mouth!" or "Those eyes go up a bit like she's happy."

How it builds self-regulation

Learning to name emotions is part of self-regulation. Children can't regulate their feelings before they can identify them by how they feel inside and by name. This activity promotes this awareness in several ways.

First, fairy tales offer representations of more complex emotions than many other picture books. They include negative emotions such as jealousy, rage, and fear that are part of a child's emotional repertoire even though we don't label and address them as frequently as happy, sad, and mad. Because children have connected emotionally to the characters in the fairy tales, they have a better sense of what the characters are feeling and why.

Second, creating the expressions connected with these emotions with playdough helps children gain mastery of the labels as they reflect on how the facial features look. They felt the emotions when they heard the story, they looked carefully at the facial expression in the illustration, they made their own face replicate that emotion and saw what it looks like in a mirror, and now they are re-creating it with a familiar material that doesn't require the abstract thinking or fine-motor skills that drawing does. And importantly, they are hearing the emotion labeled at the same time. All of this contributes to the emotional literacy that every child needs for healthy social-emotional development.

Transition Activity: Cleanup Time!

Even the most helpful classes will tire of the usual cleanup routine, which is one of the best strategies we have for promoting self-regulation as well as initiative and a sense of community in our classrooms. "Cinderella" is the perfect story to breathe a little magic into the humdrum routine. No materials are needed.

1. Teach children a new cleanup song, to the tune of "London Bridge":
   Cinderella cleans the house, cleans the house, cleans the house.
   Cinderella cleans the house . . .
   We clean our classroom!

2. Encourage the children to sing this as they clean up. Alternatively, you can sing it to announce cleanup time.

3. Add extra sparkle to the routine with a teacher-made magic wand. Go around as children are cleaning up and tap children who are working hard gently on the head with the wand, identifying what they're doing: "Zing! You are magically putting every block on the right shelf!" "Zing! I see you've shaken out all the toys in the sand table!" Giving specific descriptions of what children have done builds self-regulation and self-efficacy, and the wand helps them pay attention.

4. Wave the wand over areas that have been overlooked: "Uh-oh! I see the dramatic play area needs some sparkle. Which of my friends will make those dress-ups magically hop onto the hooks?"

5. If you have children help monitor their friends' efforts during cleanup time, encourage the monitors to use magic wands in the same way.

Hansel and Gretel: Teamwork Magic

Story Magic

A woodcutter's family is poor and doesn't have enough food. The (step)mother suggests that the woodcutter take the two children, Hansel and Gretel, out into the forest and leave them. The children overhear the plan; Hansel sneaks outside in the middle of the night and gathers white pebbles. When they are on their way to the forest, he leaves a trail behind and the brother and sister find their way home. The father tries again; this time the door is locked overnight and Hansel can't get outside to collect pebbles. Instead, Hansel leaves a trail of bread crumbs when the father takes them out to the forest. However, when they start home, they discover that birds have eaten the bread crumbs. They wander lost in the wood and come upon a house made of cookies and candy. They hungrily begin to eat it. A blind witch comes out of the house; she puts Hansel into a cage to fatten him up so she can eat him and makes Gretel cook and clean for her. They trick the witch by pretending a chicken bone is Hansel's skinny finger, which the witch checks every day as she waits for him to get plump. Finally, the witch decides she has waited long enough and she'll eat Hansel anyway. She asks Gretel to climb into the oven to see if the bread is done. Gretel asks the witch to show her how and then pushes the witch in, closes the door, and saves the day. The children discover jewels and treasure in the house, which they take home to their father, who has missed them terribly. They find that the stepmother has died while they were away.

Versions and Variants to Consider

"Hansel and Gretel" variants are told all over the world. However, very few of these appear in picture book format besides the Grimms' German version. Many versions of the classic tale are available, illustrated in just about every imaginable style. Some have minor variations: a white bird leads Hansel and Gretel to the witch's house, or a white duck or swan carries them over a river. Children will enjoy noticing these differences, as well as deciding which styles of illustration they like best.

Hansel and Gretel, retold by Rika Lesser and illustrated by Paul Zelinsky, is a Caldecott Honor book with detailed and intriguing oil paintings.

Hansel and Gretel, retold and illustrated by Jane Ray, strikes a good balance between the mysterious and the fanciful in the illustrations and feels folklorish.

Hansel and Gretel, retold and illustrated by James Marshall, features Marshall's characteristically humorous illustrations. This takes some of the edge from the story: it's hard not to laugh at a bulbous witch in a bright orange hat, even if she does want to eat you!

Hansel and Gretel, retold and illustrated by Beni Montresor, is unique not only in its paper silhouette illustrations but also because the story itself has some differences. The children get lost in the woods, but their parents have nothing to do with it: they just fall asleep after gathering and eating strawberries. Gretel also frees other children from the witch's cottage before returning home. (The witch still is burned up at the end though.)

Hansel and Gretel Stories around the World, by Cari Meister, features four simply told stories from Germany, Russia, Italy, and the Philippines. Each is illustrated in a different style, offering children multiple ways to see the relationship between brother and sister play out when they are abandoned by their parent(s).

Themes of Resilience

Many children love "Hansel and Gretel," but the fairy tale often horrifies adults when they revisit it. Starvation, child abandonment, cannibalism, and burning a witch? How could they have ever loved it? And yet they did. Some suggest it was the candy house they liked, and indeed this is a powerful image. But we aren't showing children much respect if we think they overlook all the scary parts because of a few candy canes. Perhaps it is instead the way the brother and sister overcome great odds and save each other that resonates with children. The story highlights all of the protective factors of resilience very clearly.

This inherent resilience is important to consider if children seem to be triggered by the beginning of the story. Certainly, children in our classes have felt abandoned, whether by divorce, incarceration, death in the family, or being placed in foster care. Does this mean we should avoid the story? It is up to you because you know the children in your care best. But child psychologists have long used fairy tales with children who have been traumatized because they offer satisfying resolutions to challenges.

If you notice that a child seems upset by this (or any) story, it is fine to stop and tell the children you will finish it another day, perhaps ending with a positive question like "How do you think Hansel and Gretel will find their way home? How might they feel safer in the woods?" This checks whether a child who seemed upset can articulate what was bothering them. You may ask if they'd like you to read them the story, just the two of you. This way they can tell you if they want you to stop reading and can talk to you about the scary parts. It gives you the chance to highlight the strong elements of resilience the tale explores.

Themes of Attachment and Relationships

The relationship between the brother and the sister is dominant in the story. They are forever a team, and it is through teamwork that they escape their fate. They have each other's backs from the start. In many versions, Gretel carries both pieces of bread they are given, since Hansel's pockets are filled with pebbles the first day. On their second trip into the forest, when Hansel uses his bread to leave a trail of bread crumbs, she shares her piece with him.

Most notable is how both children are active participants in the rescue and have good ideas that contribute equally to the happy ending, which is characteristic of healthy peer relationships, whether between siblings, friends, or partners.

Questions to Explore the Protective Factor of Attachment with Children

1. What are some ways that Hansel and Gretel worked together as a team?

2. When have you helped your brother or sister or a friend? How did that make you feel?

Themes of Initiative and Executive Functions

Hansel and Gretel use their wits to solve their problems. Their determination to succeed is evident in every part of the story. Even their initial gobbling of the witch's house, which we'll discuss below under Themes of Self-Regulation, is framed within the context of getting home safely: they are hungry and need strength, and they are hopeful that the occupant of the house will offer them a place to stay.

Questions to Explore the Protective Factor of Initiative with Children

1. What were some good ideas Hansel had?

2. What were some good ideas Gretel had?

3. What are some good ideas you've had that helped you solve a problem?

Themes of Self-Regulation

Hansel and Gretel demonstrate both ends of the self-regulation continuum, just as we all do. Through most of the story, they manage their stress and fear extraordinarily well. They do not freeze when they encounter multiple frights. Instead, they think calmly and clearly and come up with novel ways to get out of tough predicaments. The exception is when they eagerly start to grab the candy off the house without thinking. This lands them in more danger than before. Hansel and

Gretel are wonderful role models for children who are still working on self-regulation, showing that even if you can't stop yourself from doing something, you can regain control over the situation and things will turn out all right.

Questions to Explore the Protective Factor of Self-Regulation with Children

1. What were some times that Hansel and Gretel probably felt scared? What did they do when they were scared?

2. What do you think Hansel and Gretel thought when they saw the candy house? What did they do?

3. What was a time when you wanted to do something that maybe you thought you shouldn't? How did you stop yourself?

Additions to the Story Center

- Smelly markers. This is the perfect time to unveil a set of scented markers, most of which smell like candy.

- Candy cane–shaped pencils and candy-themed erasers (stock up around the holidays). Children often don't use pencils, especially when colorful markers and crayons are available. This invites them to give pencils a try.

- House-shaped paper. Trim white paper into a simple house shape.

- Bingo daubers. These are an inexpensive substitute for stickers for decorating stories, pictures, or houses.

Ideas for Storytelling/Storyacting

After going into the woods with Hansel and Gretel, more siblings may show up in the children's stories than usual, and they may run through a forest to get home. If the candy house appears, it's likely to become a repeated motif in future storytelling. And don't be surprised by the witch!

When a forest is the setting, remember to cast children as trees, birds, squirrels, and so on. If these are not mentioned specifically, ask the author if they would like to have children play these roles as it includes more children and lets them move as trees and forest animals. It may also inspire storytellers to add these details into their dictations.

Your storytellers might send their witches to a horrible death, which is an important way for children to gain control over things that scare them. Because of their stage of moral development, most children below the age of six or seven believe that the bad guys have to be punished for there to be justice (Piaget 1965). Rather than censuring this, consider ways to validate children's need for fairness without necessarily condoning violence. If the story has a witch being pushed into the oven, recognize that children don't yet understand the specifics of what this entails. Saying something like, "Okay, bad witch: What does it feel like if you touch something hot? Can you show us that in the oven?" will probably result in the witch saying, "Ouch ooch ouchie!" which shows the witch has been punished but also diffuses tension as the children giggle and clap.

Caring Magic
Outdoor Partner Scavenger Hunt

Children love treasure hunts, and it's even better when they are searching outside in nature! Use Hansel and Gretel's adventure to develop children's focus and inspire collaboration in this personalized scavenger hunt on your playground or sidewalk.

For each pair of children you will need:

- Scavenger hunt chart (see below)
- A cardboard "clipboard" to write on (these can be cut or torn from boxes in the recycle bin)
- Pencils or crayons
- Paper bags if you want children to collect items rather than just spot them

1. Decide how many objects you want children to find, based on the age of the children, the location of your hunt, and how much time you have. Between six and twelve items usually works well (fewer for very young children).

2. List objects children will be able to find in the designated outdoor space. Even asphalt lots have lots of natural treasures if you look! Examples of things to find: rock, leaf, flower, stick, bug, mushroom, seed, something blue, something red, something round, something square, something a bird eats, a crack, a fence, a door, and so on.

3. Create the scavenger hunt charts. This first scavenger hunt may take some time to prepare, but after you've made it, you can use the sheets repeatedly (especially if you laminate them). It is also easy to tweak a few items to vary by season. There are a number of ready-to-print generic pre-school scavenger hunts online if you don't have time to create your own.

    ○ Draw a grid with the proper number of squares (by hand or on a computer).

    ○ In each square, write the name of the object to search for and find simple clip art to match.

    ○ Print and use a paper clip to attach a copy to each cardboard "clipboard."

4. Introduce the hunt.

    ○ Explain that just like Hansel and Gretel had to use their eyes to find things in the forest, we are also going to hunt for things.

    ○ Have children choose a partner (or group of three), or assign.

    ○ Give each pair a chart on a "clipboard" and each child a pencil or crayon.

    ○ Tell them to work together, like Hansel and Gretel, to find each object. When they do, they may cross it out.

    ○ If you want to add the objects to your sensory table or discovery center, provide a paper bag for the children to collect the items.

5. Hunt!

6. Come together as a group to share their discoveries.

How it builds attachment and relationships

While young children learn to play together, they less frequently work as a team to accomplish a goal. This simple activity allows them to practice teamwork. Because children naturally pay attention to what they notice in their environment, they will appreciate each other's differences and strengths. Most children are far better observers than we are and will rely on each other to complete the task.

Brother, Come and Dance with Me

When children hear music, their bodies start to sway naturally. This simple dance invites them to explore a less familiar genre of music while supporting perspective-taking and movement play.

You will need:

- Recording of "Brother, Come and Dance with Me" song. [Note: Search online video sites for the song's title and add "for children" and you'll find performances by children's musicians instead of opera stars.]

1. Tell children the backstory: Hansel and Gretel wanted to feel less scared in the forest, so they decided to sing and dance.

2. Have the children listen to the song all the way through once or twice, making some of the motions, either seated or standing. Then they can dance as they follow the directions.

   The basic words to the song are as follows:
   > Brother, come and dance with me.
   > It's not hard, as you can see.
   > Right foot first, left foot then.
   > Then round about and back again.
   > With your head go nick nick nick;
   > With your hands you click click click.
   > Right foot first, left foot then.
   > Then round about and back again.

   Note that there are slight variations, including some versions that say, "First one foot, the other then," eliminating the left/right distinction that many preschoolers are not yet developmentally ready for.

3. Pair off "brothers" and "sisters" or have the children dance as a group.

How it builds attachment and relationships

There are few things that bring us together more joyfully than singing and dancing. When children and adults join in the fun, trust and attachment grow naturally. Think of the glee when we do the hokey pokey! Because it is embedded in a story about relationships that the children are familiar with, this song can have even more impact. Plus it's opera, giving us a quick dip into a style of music that may be unfamiliar.

Doing Magic: Playing Magic

Props for Dramatic Play

- Cookie trays
- Cookie cutters
- Bowls, spoons, and spatulas
- Various plastic baked goods or empty boxes of cookies, crackers, and cake mixes
- Aprons
- Oven mitts and hot pads

Props for Blocks/Building

- Plastic trees
- Cotton balls or small white pieces of paper
- People
- Brown construction paper, tape, and crayons to build the candy house or paper-wrapped blocks

Props for Outside Play Areas

- Cups and buckets to collect pebbles in
- Outdoor kitchen "supplies," such as spoons, bowls, cookie trays, and so on

Props for Sensory Tables

- Natural "forest" materials (for suggestions see the list in appendix A)
- Small white pebbles
- Scoops and craft sticks

Props for the Art Area

- Homemade gingerbread playdough (add ginger, cinnamon, and nutmeg to playdough)
- Cookie cutters

Props for the Math/Manipulative Center

- Pebbles
- Plastic candies
- Buttons
- Counting frames
- Cupcake liners

Props for the Discovery/Science Center

- Natural "forest" materials (for suggestions see the list in appendix A)
- Small pebbles (white or otherwise)
- Scoops and craft sticks
- Magnifying glasses
- Balance scale

Doing Magic: Making Magic
Candy Lab

There are many ways to build gingerbread houses, using graham crackers, cardboard, playdough, real candy, and so on. All of these build initiative in young children if they construct them on their own while following basic guidelines. We chose this candy-related activity instead because it also stimulates curiosity and has no specific end result.

You will need:

- A wide variety of "penny candy" (be sure to check ingredients if you have children with allergies in your class)
- Assorted spoons
- Small pitchers of water
- Funnels
- Plastic beakers (if available)
- Magnifying glasses

For each child you will need:

- Baggies of individual candies
- 1–2 small bowls and cups of different sizes
- Eyedroppers
- Large plastic tweezers
- A plastic or aluminum tray for individual "lab" space
- Plastic safety goggles (optional)
- A way to document the candy scientist's findings (paper or note cards to record observations, phone for photos or videos, and so on)

1. Set up individual lab spaces for each child to keep cross-handling of wet candies to a minimum. On each tray, place baggies of candy, several cups and bowls, an eyedropper, and tweezers.

2. Place small pitchers of water and additional shared tools in the center of the table.

3. Invite the scientists to take a seat. Introduce them to the lab where the witch makes all the candies. Their job is to investigate the candies to learn as much as they can about them.

4. Demonstrate any unfamiliar tools.

5. Help children pour water and reach tools as requested.

6. Scaffold problem solving as needed. For example, you might say, "I wonder why the Tootsie Roll stays the same shape but the Smarties get smaller?" or "Why do you think the Zotz bubbles? Does the butterscotch?"

7. Consider including taste tests as part of the scientific inquiry, and ask the children to compare the taste, smell, and texture of their concoctions.

8. Write down the children's observations. Consider constructing a class candy science book so Hansel and Gretel can tell their father all about it when they get home.

9. At the end, if permissible, allow children to "nibble, nibble like a mouse" and eat their concoctions.

How it builds initiative and executive functions

Part of problem solving is "problem finding," and in this activity children playfully examine candy in a new way, giving them lots of things to wonder about. Just as play at the sensory areas often lasts for hours, this activity may fully engage children, even those who usually don't focus on tasks for extended periods. There is something about candy (and exploring states of matter) that most children find fascinating, which helps them develop perseverance. In addition, while there are no specific end results, there *are* specific steps to follow: pick up the eyedropper, squeeze it, put it in the water, let it go, move it to the cup, and finally squeeze it again onto the candy. Working memory is actively engaged because the goals are the children's own.

Cognitive flexibility is stimulated because in the child's experience, candy is for eating—or being told not to eat. Yet now they are investigating it like scientists. They play with it, soak it in water, dissolve it, float it, and stir it into soups. As these actions follow the children's own ideas, they promote self-efficacy. It is also an exercise in effortful control; usually when you see a piece of candy, you pop it in your mouth. But a scientist hoping to uncover the witch's secrets can't do that.

Build a Witch Trap

What if instead of pushing the witch into the oven, Hansel and Gretel had built a witch trap? What would it look like? How would it work?

You will need:

- Loose parts (for suggestions see the list in appendix A)
- Attachments (for suggestions see the list in appendix A)
- Construction paper and cardboard scraps
- Markers
- Scissors
- Small dolls or "people" to test the trap
- Construction paper witch hats (optional)

1. Allow children time to tinker with the materials.
2. Ask, "How could you build a trap that would hold one of these witches?"
3. Allow children to work individually or collaboratively to build a trap.
4. Encourage children to test their traps, using the "witches."

How it builds initiative and executive functions

Tinkering and making are problem solving at its finest. Children use all of their executive function skills to create something from scratch and feel satisfied with both the *process* of trying out their own ideas and the *product*: a way to trap a witch.

Superpower Magic
Candyland

Candyland is a favorite for most young children, so open the box, get out the board and playing pieces, and let the fun (and self-regulation challenge) begin!

How it builds self-regulation

Board games are usually too complex for preschoolers, but the classic game Candyland is an exception. It does not require strategy or skill, but it does offer young children valuable experience in regulating what they think should happen (they win) with what does happen if all players follow the rules and take fair turns. If they just move to the end of the board, or don't go back spaces when they are supposed to, the game ends in a flurry of accusations and tears.

As with make-believe play, and most other kinds of play, the whole point is to continue playing. When someone's action disturbs the delicate balance of young children's interactions, the play ends. This is a powerful reason to regulate emotions and actions.

Old Mother Witch

Children love chase games, and this one engages their imaginations and bodies as they run from the witch and keep track of a jewel in this variation of Duck, Duck, Goose.

You will need:

- A penny or a plastic jewel (a large jewel is easier to handle than a penny for many children)

1. Choose one child to be the witch. Give that child a penny or jewel to hold.

2. Ask the other children to sit in a circle with their hands cupped behind their backs and their eyes closed (if possible).

3. Have the children chant the following as the witch goes around the circle:
   > Old Mother Witch!
   > Fell in a ditch!
   > Picked up a penny [jewel]
   > And thought she was rich!

4. Ask the witch to drop the penny or jewel into another child's hands. When the child feels it, they get up and chase the witch around the circle. If the witch reaches the child's spot before being caught, the child becomes the new witch.

How it builds self-regulation

The tension between knowing your turn is coming and waiting until it actually arrives can be tricky for preschoolers to balance. They have to be ready but not move. This supports self-regulation and may be one of the reasons that games like Duck, Duck, Goose are so popular. Other versions of Old Mother Witch can be found online and have similar benefits; these will add a level of challenge to this game if your class is ready.

Transition Activities

Sneaking. With Hansel sneaking out of the house and the children approaching the cottage, there is plenty of sneaking in this story. Sneaking quietly to the bathroom or outside to the playground is more engaging, and more helpful to self-regulation, than walking quietly in a line.

Following the white pebbles into or out of naptime with flashlights. While cots are being set up, or while children are resting, the teacher quietly lays a trail of pebbles. One or two children at a time follow the trail into or out of the darkened nap room, giving this sometimes difficult transition a little magic and mystery.

Pebble pickup. Children often finish with snack or a task before their friends and have to wait. Scaffold self-regulation during these times by scattering white pebbles and asking the children who are waiting to help Hansel by collecting them in small cups or baggies. Substitute items like cotton balls, pom-poms, or snips of white paper. Increase the challenge by setting a timer and seeing who can pick up the most. Alternatively, have children place all the pebbles in one basket so it becomes a collaborative effort.

Yoga for waiting. Woodchopper Pose (since Hansel and Gretel's father was a woodchopper)

- Have children stand with legs apart and hands clasped overhead.
- Have them bend slightly backward and then come slowly forward and down, letting their arms swing between their legs. Repeat ten times.

6

Rapunzel:
The Magic
of Overcoming
Obstacles

Story Magic

A man and his wife long for a child. When at last the wife becomes pregnant, she
has cravings for an herb called *rapunzel* that grows across their fence in the garden of a sorceress. Her husband sneaks into the sorceress's garden and brings his
wife the rapunzel. She devours it but wants more. The next time when the husband goes to the garden, the sorceress is there, and she demands the baby when
it is born in exchange for the rapunzel. She takes the child, names her Rapunzel,
and raises her as her own. When Rapunzel is twelve, the sorceress puts her in a
high tower with no doors. Rapunzel lets the sorceress up by tossing down her long
hair. One day a prince rides by and hears Rapunzel singing. He falls in love. He
hides until he discovers how the sorceress gets into the tower, and then he asks
Rapunzel to let down her hair for him. She does. He asks her to marry him, and
she agrees. He visits every night, and the sorceress visits during the day. One day
Rapunzel tells the sorceress that her dress has gotten tight; the sorceress realizes
that Rapunzel is with child. She cuts off her hair and throws Rapunzel out into
the wilds, where Rapunzel soon gives birth to twins. When the prince comes, the

sorceress lets him climb up Rapunzel's hair and then tells him he will never see his beloved again. He lets go of the hair and falls into thornbushes, which blind him. He wanders through the wilderness for years. One day he hears singing. It is Rapunzel. She weeps, and her tears give him back his sight. Rapunzel, the prince, and their twins go back to the prince's kingdom and live happily ever after.

Versions and Variants to Consider

Rapunzel by Rachel Isadora retells the classic story and sets it in Africa. Long blonde tresses are replaced by beaded braids, and the fabrics, plants, and animals are all inspired by Isadora's time in various African countries. Be aware that the book does not accurately represent any one region in Africa and is not an "African" variant of "Rapunzel." However, between her large and colorful pictures and the clear text, this version is excellent for all ages and for group and individual readings.

Rapunzel by Paul Zelinsky won a Caldecott Medal. Zelinsky draws on Renaissance art for his inspiration, and both the detail and the fairy tale–like imagery are engaging.

Rapunzel from the Once upon a World series (written by Chloe Perkins, illustrated by Archana Sreenivason, in board book format) is set in India. The story line is similar, but this version adds Rapunzel's longing to see the world, and Rapunzel and the Prince do not have children.

The Canary Prince, an Italian version of "Rapunzel," can be found in anthologies and as a picture book by Eric Jon Nones. Because it is longer and the story line is more complex, it is better suited for children in the primary grades. The girl in the tower demonstrates tremendous problem-solving skills and initiative, so it's an excellent way to get children discussing these aspects of resilience. Preschool teachers who want to share it could break it into shorter episodes and read these on successive days.

Themes of Attachment and Relationships

The relationships in "Rapunzel" are complicated, much like real-life relationships. As in many fairy tales, Rapunzel's parents give her up, although they don't want to. All versions show their love for their baby daughter. While we can peg the sorceress or witch as cruel, when we read the story, it's clear that she raises Rapunzel with kindness and makes sure that she has everything she needs, even in the tower. As such, she acts as a competent adult, in addition to a parental figure. Rapunzel and the prince's friendship, which turns into love, is a good example of peer relationships. They enjoy each other's company in the tower, and when they are both cast out, they continue to look for each other until they are reunited.

Questions to Explore the Protective Factor of Attachment with Children

1. Look at the pictures of Rapunzel when she was with the sorceress. What do you think the sorceress did to make Rapunzel feel loved?

2. Rapunzel's tears helped the prince see again. How do you think that happened?

Themes of Initiative and Executive Functions

While it's easy to see Rapunzel as passively waiting in the tower for her prince, this is not so. She sings while in the tower, showing her self-efficacy. In several versions, Rapunzel or the prince works on a rope ladder to solve the problem of getting her down. Both Rapunzel and the prince also demonstrate motivation to succeed as they survive in the wilderness.

Questions to Explore the Protective Factor of Initiative with Children

1. Rapunzel was alone in the tower a lot. What do you play when you are by yourself to keep yourself happy?

2. What do you think was the bravest thing Rapunzel did? What was the bravest thing the prince did?

Themes of Self-Regulation

There is little more difficult for young children than waiting for something they enjoy! Rapunzel demonstrates this daily, as she waits for the sorceress and the prince. The prince, too, demonstrates self-regulation in a way that children can relate to. He hides quietly and watches the tower to see how someone can get in. On the other hand, the sorceress demonstrates a lack of self-regulation when she discovers Rapunzel's visitor: she immediately cuts off Rapunzel's hair in a rage and casts her into the wild. Often we see this kind of impulsive behavior in the villains in fairy tales (think of "Rumpelstiltskin," for example). Reflecting on the sorceress's impulsive behavior can help children become more aware of their own emotions and actions.

Questions to Explore the Protective Factor of Self-Regulation with Children

1. What do you do when you are feeling impatient or have to wait for something, like Rapunzel waited for the sorceress every day?

2. The prince hid quietly so he could see how to get into the tower. What are some times during our day here at school when you have to wait quietly before you get something you want?

3. What did the sorceress do when she discovered that Rapunzel had become friends with the prince? What do you think she was feeling? What have you done when you've been very angry at a friend?

Additions to the Story Center

- Light gray construction paper
- Paper printed with a brick texture (search online for patterns to print)
- Small, washable blocks or brick-textured stamps with stamp pads
- Textured papers, wallpaper samples, and cardboard to cut into shapes and add to picture stories

- Child-made tissue paper collages to cut up (see page 77 for ideas about how to create these nonrepresentational art collage papers)

- Envelopes and postage-stamp stickers in case Rapunzel wants to write to her parents, the sorceress, or the prince

Ideas for Storytelling/Storyacting

Children enjoy acting out inanimate objects as well as humans and animals. "Rapunzel" has some fascinating "noncharacters," including the tower. If your version features a tower, invite the children to decide how many actors it will take to make it. Then allow them to figure out how to create it with their bodies. This promotes mental imagery, body awareness, and collaborative problem solving. Other images that might figure in children's stories and can be acted out include the braid, the thorny bush the prince falls on, and the twin babies (preschoolers, especially, love to pretend to be babies and will sometimes add them to stories for just this purpose).

Caring Magic
Class Tower Mural

This group mural of a tower is a collaborative class project that even very young children can easily help to build. Watching it grow higher, and higher, and even higher is part of the fun.

You will need:

- Bulletin board or other long paper

- A variety of art materials: construction paper, newspaper or magazine clippings, markers, paint, nature materials, and so forth

- Books with pictures of towers for reference

1. Select a wall or bulletin board where a tall tower can be displayed.

2. Cut paper to desired height. Older children can help measure the paper to fit the display space.

3. As a class, decide how to create the tower. Depending on the age of the children, this might be construction paper "bricks" or "stones," cut or torn and decorated with markers or paint; nature collage materials like moss, sticks, and leaves; torn newspaper or magazine "blocks"; or tower bricks painted or drawn directly onto the background.

4. Have children work in small groups over several days to construct the tower at a table or directly on the wall or bulletin board, depending on the height of the tower and materials used.

5. Encourage children to reference pictures of towers and discuss details such as where the window will be, whether there should be a door, how close together blocks should be, and so on.

6. Use the finished tower as a backdrop for reading a Rapunzel story.

How it builds attachment and relationships

Many young children are used to working alone on art projects. A tower is the ideal subject for a class mural because it is large enough for many children to collaborate. Letting the children decide on the materials and methods of creating the tower encourages them to share their different visions. Working in small groups to make bricks nurtures conversation. Sharing the sense of accomplishment in creating something large helps all children feel included and supported.

Rapunzel Braid Tug-of-War

This activity uses what children have learned about the strength of Rapunzel's amazing braid to engage them in big-body play as they learn social skills.

You will need:

- Rope (various materials can be used for the rope—it must be strong enough not to break when tugged but not so stiff that it hurts children's hands, like cotton clotheslines or jump ropes)

- Soft surface such as grass

1. Divide the children into two teams. Team numbers depend on the age of the children and the strength and length of the rope. In general, for preschoolers, small teams work best. Include an adult on at least one side.

2. For older children, identify a spot where the rope must be pulled to "bring the prince in." For younger children, this is not necessary but may add to the fun.

3. Have teams face each other, holding onto the rope, and pull in opposite directions. The team that pulls the other team over the spot identified is declared the "Rapunzel Strong-Hair Team" (or a name they make up).

How it builds attachment and relationships

Young children have a hard time *decentering*, or recognizing that others have a different point of view than they do, including their understanding of the physical space that others occupy. Working together physically to accomplish a common goal requires them to become more aware of each other as well as communicate with each other. In addition, most young children enjoy working hard physically and tumbling into a pile at the end of a game, which builds camaraderie, especially for children who are not as verbal as their peers.

Doing Magic: Playing Magic

Props for Dramatic Play

- Yarn braids of all colors and lengths (child-made, for older children)
- Different shades of green construction paper to tear into rapunzel; plastic play food greens (lettuce, spinach) may also be used
- Large refrigerator-sized box for children to decorate as a "tower"; cut a secret door for access and a window at shoulder height

Props for Blocks/Building and STEM

- Flat bases such as boards or trays for building higher towers
- Cardboard or other large blocks
- Yarn, rope, and string
- Simple pulleys
- Multiple yardsticks to measure towers (for older children)
- Premeasured lengths of string for nonstandard measuring
- Unifix cubes and other nonstandard measuring materials
- Stepstool so children can build higher towers, depending on age of children and comfort level of teacher

Props for Outside Play Areas

- Gardening tools
- Ropes of various lengths and thicknesses

Props for Sensory Tables

- Waterwheel beach toys that can be adapted into towers by adding braided yarn, shoelaces, string, and so forth
- Small figures
- Plastic dolls and eyedroppers (to make tears)

Doing Magic: Making Magic
Tower Power

Just as the many illustrators of this story have creatively represented the tower, children will be captivated by imagining the many ways towers can be built and then making their own. This activity should extend over multiple days.

You will need:

- Classroom materials that children can use for building

1. Challenge children to brainstorm ideas about towers that are "the most" (for example, the most high, the most wide, the most crooked, the most covered with flowers, the most sweet, or the most cardboard). Children might design the inside of a tower, so Rapunzel's room might be "the most purple," and so on.

2. Record the children's ideas. Include a list of classroom materials they think they may need. Older children can write their ideas in a journal or on a wall chart.

3. Ask the children to build their towers in the block area, art area, or other suitable space. Remember that children often need time to hatch great ideas. Adding interesting materials to the block area, as described previously, may spur creativity.

4. Set up a special area to display the towers as they are completed (this can serve as a place to store them between building sessions as well). Have children write or dictate labels for their creations. Encourage children to discuss each other's ideas.

How it builds initiative and executive functions

Towers fascinate most children. Offering them the chance to create their own inspires problem solving and persistence, since building a tower comes with a built-in set of balance and engineering challenges. Connecting the project with "Rapunzel," with its dominant tower theme, helps children to draw on their own

mental representations of a tower and encourages them to make a structure that is unique. Adding the "most" parameter further engages their imagination, and through it, their self-efficacy.

Nonrepresentational Art Collage Papers

Rachel Isadora's collage artwork inspires this activity. Like many other illustrators, she cuts shapes out of richly textured papers to create pictures. Children can make their own collage papers, which can be put in the story center or art center to create illustrations. This activity can occur on one day, with multiple stations set up simultaneously, or over several days, with just one selection of materials available each day. The ratio of adults to children and their ages will determine this.

You will need:

- Paper to collage on (preschoolers may do best with 9" x 12" white construction paper cut into half or even quarters so they decorate each paper fully)

- Medium to create collage papers, such as:

  ○ Torn tissue paper and water glue

  ○ Bingo daubers

  ○ Tempera paint prints: cover paper with impressions, using objects like lids, buttons, bread tags, spools, toilet paper rolls, and so on

  ○ Crayon rubbings (bark, leaves, cloth, and so on)

  ○ Marble rolling: Place a piece of paper in the lid from a shoe box and add a little tempera paint and several marbles; children tip the lid from side to side to roll marbles and cover paper with "tracks"

  ○ Fingerpaints

  ○ Watercolor washes

1. Set up stations with a variety of materials.

2. With children's help, assemble "collage paper books" by stapling three to five papers together. Place in the story center or art area to cut up when making collages or illustrating stories.

3. Offer inspiration with picture books that feature collage illustrations (for example, Isadora, Eric Carle, Leo Lionni, Ezra Jack Keats, and so on).

How it builds initiative and executive functions

Children develop self-efficacy when they experiment and take risks, and creating nonrepresentational art offers them this chance. Free from the constraints of a piece that "looks like" something, children act on their own ideas and become more inventive as they explore various media. This self-efficacy continues as they select from the finished papers to illustrate their own stories. This process also taps into problem solving and motivation to succeed as children cut out and assemble the papers to construct objects. Seeing themselves as artists and authors who use the same techniques as the people who made their favorite books helps children believe they are competent readers and writers, even when they have not yet formally begun to read.

Superpower Magic
The Sorceress Is Coming/The Sorceress Is Gone

This adaptation of Red Light, Green Light can be played outside or in a large room, such as a gym or gross-motor room. No materials are required, although you may want to mark both the start line and the place where Rapunzel or the prince stand with tape on the floor to cue young children.

1. Ask the children to line up at the back of the room or playground. Across the space they face one child who is designated Rapunzel or the prince.

2. When Rapunzel (or the prince) shouts, "The sorceress is coming," have the children stand completely still and "hide" (depending on age, perhaps crouching down like the prince or covering their faces with their hands).

3. When Rapunzel shouts "The sorceress is gone!" have the children walk/run toward Rapunzel (or the prince), until Rapunzel/the prince shouts, "The sorceress is coming," again.

4. Let the first child to reach Rapunzel be the new Rapunzel, and repeat the game.

How it builds self-regulation

To play this and many other common children's games, children must listen attentively and be ready to frameshift, or change what they are doing, on cue, which develops their physical self-regulation (inhibitory control). This game variation adds the element of pretending to hide on top of the basic action of

suddenly stopping one's movement, making it a bit more complex and also engaging children's imagination to support other self-regulation skills as they tap into all that hiding entails (being "small," staying quiet, and so on).

"Rapunzel's Tower Is Falling Down"

This adaptation of the childhood favorite "London Bridge" has children singing and swaying as they help to catch and then free Rapunzel.

1. Select two children to be the tower. Ask them to stand facing each other, holding hands, with their arms high up over their heads.

2. Ask the other children to line up.

3. Encourage the children to sing the following song (to the tune of "London Bridge") while they are walking through the tower:

   Rapunzel's tower is falling down,
   Falling down, falling down!
   Rapunzel's tower is falling down
   Now she's free-ee!

4. When the song gets to "Now she's free-ee," have the tower gently close on the child who is going through.

5. As the tower gently rocks the captured child back and forth, sing the second verse with the children:

   Take the key and lock her up
   Lock her up, lock her up!
   Take the key and lock her up
   She's back in here.

6. Ask the captured child to replace one half of the tower and repeat the game.

How it builds self-regulation

Children are often discouraged from doing big-body or rough-and-tumble play in classroom settings, yet these are excellent ways to develop self-regulation. If children are too rough, the game ends because someone is hurt or in trouble. Children self-regulate so play can continue. This version of "London Bridge" has the added element of a sympathetic "captive," another reason for children to self-regulate and be gentle swinging a friend back and forth.

Transition Activity: "Climbing the Braid"

Walking quietly to the bathroom or playground is a test of self-regulation for many children. After reading "Rapunzel," try using the imagery of "climbing the braid quietly" to scaffold their efforts. Set the stage by saying, "We are going to pretend to be the prince, climbing up Rapunzel's braid as quietly and carefully as we can!" Demonstrate a simple hand-over-hand climbing movement, either above your head or in front of you if space permits. You or the line leader leads the "climbing" children silently to the bathroom. This transition activity offers children something to engage their imaginations and more easily regulates their urge to run and talk because they are on a mission: to climb the braid without alerting the sorceress!

Jack and the Beanstalk: The Magic of Being Brave

Story Magic

A poor widow lives with her son, Jack, and their white cow. The family survives by selling the cow's milk. One day the cow stops giving milk and the mother tells Jack to take the cow to sell at the market. Along the way, he meets a man who offers him five magic beans for the cow. He makes the trade and returns home, and his angry mother sends him to bed without supper. She hurls the beans out the window in frustration.

The next morning, a beanstalk stretches to the sky. Jack climbs up and discovers a castle where a giant and his wife live. He asks for food; the wife tells him he'll be the giant's dinner if he doesn't leave. Finally, she gives him a bit of bread and cheese, and while he is eating it, they hear the giant. The wife hides Jack in the oven as the giant comes home, saying, "Fee Fi Foe Fum! I smell the blood of an Englishman!" The wife tells him he smells the boy he ate the day before, and he settles down to dinner.

After dinner the giant counts his gold and falls asleep. Jack sneaks out, grabs the gold, and hurries down the beanstalk, presenting the gold to his mother, who is overjoyed. All is well.

After a while, Jack climbs the beanstalk again. This time he discovers that the giant has a hen that lays golden eggs. When the giant falls asleep, Jack sneaks out of hiding and grabs the hen, whose squawking wakes up the giant. Jack barely makes it down the beanstalk with the hen. He and his mother live well.

Jack returns a third time and hides. After dinner the giant gets out a magical harp, which sings him to sleep. When Jack grabs the harp, it sings out to the giant, who chases Jack down the beanstalk. Jack yells to his mother to get an ax, he chops down the beanstalk, and he and his mother live happily ever after.

Versions and Variants to Consider

Jack and the Beanstalk, retold and illustrated by Steven Kellogg, offers detailed and lively illustrations that give children lots to look at as they hear of Jack's adventures.

Jack and the Beanstalk, retold and illustrated by Paul Galdone, is told in rhyme, giving it an extra boost for circle times, especially after the children are familiar with the story.

Kate and the Beanstalk, written by Mary Pope Osborne and illustrated by Giselle Potter, has a female hero named Kate. It includes a plot twist found in some of the oldest folk versions of the tale: the giant actually stole the castle and treasures from Kate's father when she was a baby.

Jack and the Beanstalk, retold and illustrated by Nina Crews, is set in a modern cityscape; Jack receives magic beans for helping his neighbor with chores. The collage illustrations imaginatively combine photographs to retell the story, with some curious twists that children will find funny if they already know the tale.

Themes of Attachment and Relationships

The primary relationship in this story is the one between Jack and his mother, which most young children understand. It is his mother who asks Jack to take the cow to market, his mother who is upset when he comes home with beans, his mother who throws the beans out the window (in many versions), his mother who is so delighted with Jack's treasures, and his mother who rushes to get the ax.

Even though the story is set in the fantastical world of fairy tales, the ways Jack and his mother interact are very relatable. Preschoolers want to please their moms, and like Jack, they are sometimes surprised when their best efforts make their mothers frown. While preschoolers can't make things right by climbing a magic beanstalk and showering their moms with treasures, how often do they thrust a handful of dandelions into their mother's hands or draw a special picture when they want to make up for something they've done?

Other elements of Jack's relationship with his mom resonate as well. Children whose families are struggling financially often wish they could fix things. Think of the three-year-old who finds a penny on the sidewalk and proudly presents it to "pay your bills." Similarly, children living with single parents will find the way Jack and his mom create a home and family together comforting.

The giant's wife also provides young children with a model of the competent, helpful adult. She is fierce, and she discusses cooking children, but she also feeds Jack and hides him when the giant comes home. Young children are beginning to trust relationships with adults who are not their parents as they make their way into the world. How reassuring that even in a giant's castle in the clouds there are adults who will help!

Questions to Explore the Protective Factor of Attachment with Children

1. What do you suppose Jack thought his mother would say when he brought home magic beans instead of money for the cow?

2. What do you like to do to make your family happy?

3. Why do you think the giant's wife helped Jack hide?

Themes of Initiative and Executive Functions

Jack exemplifies the protective factor of initiative. He leaps at the chance to trade the cow for magic beans, he immediately climbs the beanstalk, and he doesn't hesitate when the giant falls asleep. Jack has a problem to solve: how to help his mother afford food. He is resourceful and brave, and he does what is necessary to make the situation right after he sees his mother is not pleased about his trade.

We want this self-efficacy for all young children, as we know that it makes for strong, independent adults. Yet this desire often conflicts with our need to protect children, especially in group care and education settings. A growing body of research shows that children need to be able to act on their own ideas and take risks (physical, social, and cognitive) in supportive environments to develop confidence and learn to deal with disappointment (see, for example, Green 2017). This is true of all children, but especially children who have experienced trauma. Trying new things and being brave in a nurturing environment helps children experience a tingle of stress from the unknown without their stress responses kicking into overdrive.

Questions to Explore the Protective Factor of Initiative with Children

1. What do you think was Jack's best idea? What did you like about it?

2. Tell me about a time when you think Jack was really scared.

3. Was there a time when you did something brave when you were scared? How did it turn out? How did you feel after?

Themes of Self-Regulation

While it's easy to view Jack as a foolhardy and impulsive young boy (not even telling his mom when he clambered up the beanstalk the first time!), he is a role model for self-regulation. All young children have been asked to stay very quiet at times; they know well how difficult this is. But imagine if you had to stay quiet so the giant wouldn't eat you! While there are sadly some children who have had to hide to stay safe, most children will still relate to how hard it must have been for Jack to stay silent and then calmly sneak up to take the giant's treasures three times.

Jack demonstrates both kinds of self-regulation. He regulates his actions (talking, moving around, and so on) while hiding and regulates his emotions when he sneaks up to the giant and when the giant wakes and chases him. What if Jack yelled in surprise when the hen squawked at the giant? Instead, he self-regulates and escapes swiftly, staying focused on his goal.

Young children can't develop self-regulation without first being able to identify their own feelings—how can you control something that you don't know is there? While identifying feelings from facial expressions on flash cards is a common practice in preschools, helping children consider the feelings of characters in stories offers a more relatable context. Fairy tales like "Jack and the Beanstalk" are wonderful to use, since the characters' emotions are rarely described or labeled and children can reflect on how they might feel in similar circumstances.

Questions to Explore the Protective Factor of Self-Regulation with Children

1. What do you think Jack was thinking and feeling when he was hiding in the oven?

2. How do you think Jack felt when the hen and then the magic harp woke up the giant? What do you do when you are startled by a sudden noise?

Additions to the Story Center

Make a giant's treasure chest to store story center items. Seek examples of treasure chests made out of repurposed boxes online if you need inspiration.

Fill the treasure chest with:

- Crayons and markers in story-related colors: green (beanstalk), blue and white (sky and clouds, the white cow), gray (castle), and gold. The goal is not to get children to replicate the story but to encourage them to imagine their drawing and writing in new ways by limiting the choice of colors.

- "Giant" paper: Roll long strips of paper of various sizes and types and tie loosely with green ribbon or yarn.

- Lengths of green yarn to decorate stories or tie pages into books

- Rubber stamps of story-related items and stamp pads of various colors

- Shiny stickers of various shapes and sizes. Some children will cover the whole page with stickers if allowed, so you may want to help children conserve (and develop math skills) by giving each child five stickers.

Ideas for Storytelling/Storyacting

The images of the beanstalk, the giant, and the chase all align with young children's developmental interests. Often preschoolers have a fascination with height and high things. If the beanstalk, the giant, and the castle up high in the clouds figure as motifs in children's stories, they may enjoy prompts such as "Can you be a beanstalk as it's growing?" or "Show me how you'd climb a beanstalk. Think about climbing up our slide." Depending on the story, the children may act out being a beanstalk and being the climber. Setting boundaries such as "Remember just to pretend to touch the beanstalk; we don't want to grab our friends and accidentally hurt them" may be appropriate, depending on the age and energy level of the children.

If the castle is a main character, say to the children, "Think of the castle in the pictures. Can you make your body high and pointy like the turret?" Ask them to show they are perched high up in the clouds. Helping children tap into their imaginations promotes the mental imagery that is foundational for literacy.

The giant and the chase are both fascinating parts of this story. Young children may consider the giant a metaphor for all those adults who are bigger and more powerful than they are; telling a story that includes one may offer a bit of control. Or they may just like stomping around, saying, "Fee Fi Foe Fum!" If, after a few storyacting sessions, you find that the giant's sole role is providing noise and comic relief, consider asking questions to expand the author's thinking as they dictate their story: "What do you think the giant is going after?" "What made the giant so cranky?" and so on. These clarifying questions support young children in thinking about story structure without diminishing their ownership of the story.

You'll likely find some good chases in children's stories and chase games on the playground after reading this fairy tale. In addition to the pure joy running holds for many children, chase games are popular because children feel the thrill of anticipation when they both want to and don't want to get caught. This momentary tingle of safe stress builds our capacity for maintaining self-regulation when there are challenges.

There are ways of storyacting chase scenes that preserve classroom order and safety. If you outline the story circle in tape, remind children that all action has to take place inside the circle before any chases begin. Encourage children to run and chase in place: "We want to make sure the giant doesn't stomp on our friends. Can you use your body to pretend to run fast but really stay still?" Prompt the children as they prepare to act out the story, or include the reminders as part of your own storytelling or movement activities at a separate circle time. Think about how many motions and ways of chasing are acted out in the familiar "Bear

Hunt" story. Modeling such movements as you sing, tell stories, or do fingerplays offers children ideas for acting out chase scenes in their stories while keeping everyone safe and enthralled.

Caring Magic
Painting the Classroom Bravery Beanstalk

When children collaborate to create a strong visual for their classroom like this giant beanstalk, the community feeling empowers them to feel like they can do anything. This creation is also used for another activity that highlights children's strengths (see "Climbing the Classroom Bravery Beanstalk" on page 88).

You will need:

- A long piece of bulletin board or craft paper with a beanstalk lightly sketched on (add extra at both ends to make painting and cutting easier)
- Green paint
- Pie pans or other flat containers
- Assortment of paint daubers and interesting paintbrushes (for example, sponges cut into shapes, dish sponges on handles, mesh shower/bath "poofs")
- Newspapers or tarp to protect floor (or take the project outside)
- Paint smocks

1. Ask the children to paint the beanstalk. Depending on the length of the beanstalk and the maturity level of the children, you may want to have as few as two children working at the same time or as many as five or six (or more).

2. Allow each child to choose their paint daubers/sponges. Model using novel tools as necessary.

3. Make sure each child has their own space along the beanstalk, although sharing paint tins encourages a sense of community. Encourage children to notice what their friends are doing and how it is the same as or different from their own painting. Staying in the lines is not essential: excess paint on the beanstalk can be trimmed off.

4. After the beanstalk has dried, trim it and put it up on the wall. This can be done with great ceremony as the children watch or after they have left for the day. Imagine their wonder when they walk in the next morning and a beanstalk has grown in their classroom!

How it builds attachment and relationships

We know that young children have a hard time decentering, or being aware of each other because of their egocentrism, a developmental characteristic of preschoolers. By working together to create a beanstalk, they are sharing an experience that builds community: it will be *our* beanstalk, instead of *my* beanstalk. Because this activity entails multiple children working simultaneously, they must pay close attention to each other in physical space. By trusting that they will pay attention and not bump or paint a friend, we provide them a way to practice this critical skill of decentering. Encouraging children to pay attention to how their friends are painting increases their interest and motivation to decenter and lays the foundation for this important skill.

Climbing the Classroom Bravery Beanstalk

The magnificent beanstalk the children created in the previous activity now becomes a showcase for their own brave and daring actions and a way to validate each other as well.

You will need:

- Full-body picture of each child
- Basket
- Bravery Beanstalk (see previous activity on page 87)
- Fastener such as clothespins, sticky tack, Velcro, or masking tape

1. Collect or create a full-body picture of each child (photographs or children's self-portraits, or a mixed-media combination) and place in a basket.

2. Reintroduce the Bravery Beanstalk, which the children painted and created previously.

3. Ask the children to remember the brave things Jack did in the story.

4. Show the children the picture basket where "all of the brave children in the class have been sleeping."

5. Ask if anyone has ever done something brave, or done something even if it was hard, or done something they didn't think they could do.

6. When a child shares something, hang their picture on the beanstalk. (Children may do this themselves, but they might not get very high.) This activity can be done one time, or it can become part of your classroom routine. The brave beanstalk climbers can be taken down every night and new acts of bravery shared each day.

7. Consider asking children to nominate their friends for acts of bravery once they get the hang of the activity. Families and teachers can also make nominations.

How it builds attachment and relationships

Whether the children nominate their own acts of bravery or those of their friends, or whether adults nominate them, this activity helps children see themselves as part of a community of helpers who take risks to make things better. When children nominate themselves, other children get insight into the kinds of challenges their friends are facing and overcoming, which builds empathy. When children nominate each other, they are paying attention to each other's actions and emotions. When families and teachers make nominations, adults can reflect on and celebrate the resilience our littlest ones show every day. And we all know that children cherish the opportunity to be recognized by those they love.

Doing Magic: Playing Magic
Props for Dramatic Play

- "Giant shoes" (any adult-sized shoes or boots)
- Vests, long skirts, aprons, and other dress-ups inspired by the illustrations
- Stuffed cows
- A treasure chest
- Plastic "golden" eggs
- Simple harps or similar musical instruments (these can be made from cereal boxes and rubber bands or string)

Props for Blocks/Building and STEM

- Unit blocks wrapped in green construction paper for building beanstalks
- Large cardboard blocks—try removing all the regular blocks and just leave out the largest
- Farm animals
- Green chenille stems to twist into beanstalks
- Fluffy white bath rug or polyester filling for building castles in the clouds
- Books on castles

Props for Outside Play Areas

- If you have an outside area that can be planted or a sunny windowsill, introduce children to gardening by planting beans. Even if the vines don't produce beans, they are exciting to care for and watch grow.

- Wrap the sides of monkey bars, climbing apparatuses, play lofts, and playground ladders with green yarn or crepe paper to inspire timid climbers.

- Add castle toys and farm animals to sand areas.

- Consider allowing children to climb up the slide during specific times. This is terrific for gross-motor skills and builds initiative and agency, as well as providing "safe risk."

Props for Sensory Tables

- Shaving cream for clouds
- Duplos, Legos, or foam blocks for building castles in the clouds
- Farm animals
- Small people figures
- Green Unifix cubes

Doing Magic: Making Magic
Unifix Cubes to the Sky

This super-tall building and measuring activity works best as a partner or a small-group activity.

You will need:

- As many green Unifix cubes as you can gather
- Other colors of Unifix cubes (start with brown, blue, and white, and then add others as needed)
- Floor space that allows for building long lines of Unifix cubes
- Other building materials as desired

1. Ask the children if they could build a beanstalk that stretches to the sky. How many Unifix cubes would it take? How high would it need to go? Record their answers.

2. Show the children an area where they can build and provide Unifix cubes sorted by color (or ask the children to sort them).

3. As they snap them together, listen for problem posing as well as problem solving, such as "We're out of green, so what color comes next?" "Where should the brown ones go, at the top, or the bottom?" "How are we going to get these to stand up?"

4. When the children have either tired of building or run out of cubes, ask how they think they could measure them. How could they count them?

    ○ Nonstandard measurements (such as walking heel to toe alongside the line or using blocks or yarn to measure) are more developmentally appropriate for preschoolers than rulers. Older children might enjoy placing multiple rulers down or using a tape measure.

    ○ Counting a large number is tough, especially since many young children don't yet have a solid grasp of one-to-one correspondence. However, if they can rote count, allow them to do so, touching the cubes. It may not be accurate, but it will give them practice, and when children come up with different numbers, it's a great opportunity to recount!

    ○ Older children might enjoy learning how to make tally marks or counting by tens to keep track of their counting.

5. After the children have measured or counted their beanstalk, ask the children for their ideas to make it stand up. Have materials ready to support their solutions, such as masking tape, yarn, cardboard, and so forth.

6. If children can't figure it out—taking apart the cubes and rebuilding may be too heartbreaking of an option—remind them of the end of the story, when the beanstalk has been chopped down.

7. Ask the children to pull apart the beanstalk (see how fast they can do so) and turn it back into "magic beans" for cleanup.

How it builds initiative and executive functions

There is something very satisfying about building the biggest, the longest, or the highest. This activity allows children to work in a context from a story they've been immersed in. As they generate and discuss solutions to problems, they are using the executive function of cognitive flexibility. For example, if they run out of green cubes, one child may suggest using brown or gray like the castle, then a friend might say they should put the brown ones at the bottom of the beanstalk (like dirt). In the hands of engaged children, even a simple problem like this can spark discussion that promotes cognitive flexibility.

The executive function of working memory also comes into play during this activity. For younger children, putting the cubes together into such a long beanstalk may challenge them to stay focused on the steps of the task. More skilled builders may be challenged instead by counting and measuring and then recording their progress.

Finally, a look at children's faces after they have co-created such a long structure is all one needs to recognize mastery motivation. Young children are immensely satisfied when they create something that was not there before. A child-directed project such as this one can provide even children who participate peripherally or for a short time a great sense of accomplishment.

Golden Egg Hunt

In this activity, children use clues to find hidden golden eggs laid by the giant's hen.

You will need:

- Plastic eggs painted gold
- Picture and/or word clues for where the eggs are hidden (prepared ahead of time by a teacher or with a small group of children)
- Basket for eggs (optional)

1. Create the clues. They can be photographs of areas of the room or playground; symbols for centers that the children are familiar with, such as Picture Exchange Communication System (PECS) icons; or written clues the teacher will read. (Rhyming clues are fun and build phonemic awareness but are not necessary.)

2. Put aside the first clue. Then hide the other eggs in the locations you've identified, being sure to put a clue that does *not* match its egg's location inside each of the golden eggs.

3. Tell children that the giant's hen came to visit and laid eggs all over the classroom or playground, and Jack and his mother need help finding them.

4. Read the first clue or show the children the picture. Before they charge off to find it, ask them to share ideas about where the egg could be. For example, if the picture shows the block area, ask, "Where could a hen lay an egg in the block area?"

5. After children guess, ask them to tiptoe over (so as not to disturb the hen or the giant) and look. When a child finds an egg, they may call out, "Fee Fi Foe Fum! I found an egg, so everyone come!" Then they may open the egg for the next clue.

6. Ask the children to put the eggs in the basket with the clues back inside. This repeats until all the eggs are found. Note: Consider making a master clue sheet before cutting the clues apart so the activity can be repeated even if a clue or two goes missing. A master clue sheet can also serve as a "map" to model using maps with children if they can't find an egg.

How it builds initiative and executive functions

We all know the thrill of finding something lost (especially if it's our lost keys!) and the sense of accomplishment it brings. Children feel satisfied twice: once when they (or a friend) guess what the clue means, and again when that idea leads them to the egg. This promotes both cognitive flexibility and a sense of agency.

The activity can be adapted for younger learners by using fewer eggs; adapt it for more mature children (especially useful in mixed-age groups or where older children share a playground with younger ones) by giving them control over hiding the eggs and crafting the clues. The hiders can take ownership for setting up a great hunt, and the seekers feel pride in solving the clues and discovering the eggs.

Superpower Magic
Hide-and-Go-Seek, Jack Style

This twist on hide-and-seek captures all the thrill and learning of the original with an additional *Rraarrrr* or two!

1. Discuss what children remember about how Jack hid at the giant's house. How did he keep from getting discovered?

2. Identify a child to be the giant.

3. Ask the other children to hide as the "giant" counts to an age-appropriate number. When the countdown is over, have the giant call, "Fee Fi Foe Fum! I am the giant, and here I come!"

4. Ask the giant to describe what they see when they find another child, for example, "I see Jimmy's feet sticking out from the bush." Children with less developed verbal skills or who are dual language learners can make a giant face and say, "*Rraarrrr*" or "Fee Fi Foe Fum," or touch a hiding child lightly on the shoulder.

5. Ask the child who is discovered to become the next giant, and repeat the game.

How it builds self-regulation

There are lots of reasons why young (and not so young) children love to play hide-and-seek, including the thrills of discovering *and* being discovered. Hide-and-seek is also wonderful self-regulation practice. Both the children who are hiding and the "giant" must exert control over their impulse to talk, move, and peek—much easier in the context of play than when sitting in circle time. Adding story elements to the traditional game actively engages children's imaginations, and research has shown that children exhibit higher levels of self-regulation during pretend play than almost any other time (see, for example, Leong and Bodrova 2012).

The suggestion to have the "giant" describe what they see when they find a child adds scaffolding for young children who wonder why they are always the first to be discovered and are less inclined to stay still as a result. In hide-and-seek, young children often assume that if they can't see anyone coming, no one can see them. By having the giant describe what they see, children begin to realize that others see them from a different perspective. They thus can more effectively hide and self-regulate the next time.

Magic Lyre Freeze Dance

This is an adaptation of another childhood favorite, freeze dance.

You will need:

- Music (harp or lyre music is ideal since it ties into the story and children are often unfamiliar with this type of music)

- Device or mechanism to play the music so the music can be easily started and stopped

1. Play a little bit of the music while the children are sitting and have them imagine they are in the giant's castle listening to his magical lyre.

2. Explain that they will need to quietly walk, dance, or creep around the castle, and when the music stops, they have to freeze in place, since the giant might wake up.

3. Start the music, motion for the children to get up and start to move, and soon stop the music. Notice who is "frozen." If children aren't still, encourage them to freeze now (since the giant isn't awake yet . . . whew!).

4. Repeat until the children tire of the game or the music ends.

How it builds self-regulation

This freeze dance removes the competition and the physical coordination of musical chairs to focus just on listening to the music, moving, and then stopping, requiring children to pay close attention while they are moving and frameshift from dancing to being still very quickly.

As in the hide-and-seek activity, adding the connection to the story engages children's imaginations and supports their developing self-regulation skills. Stopping when the music stops is fun; stopping when the magical lyre stops so the giant won't notice you is purposeful and exciting!

Transition Activities

Climbing the beanstalk. This movement helps children travel from one activity or area to another, especially when they have to stay in line. Ask the children to practice "climbing" by raising one arm and then another before adding their feet. For most preschoolers, just regular walking is enough of a challenge, as moving their upper body separately from their lower body is tricky. This kind of movement is not only fun but also requires focus and self-regulation, especially as children are moving down a hall.

Tiptoe like Jack. Our hero Jack is quiet so he won't get caught! Ask children to tiptoe as they "sneak" from one activity to another.

Thumbelina and Tom Thumb:
Tiny and Resilient Magic

Story Magic

A couple wishes for a child, even if the child is "no bigger than a thumb." A tiny child is born and deeply loved. As the child grows older, the child either has great desire to explore the world (usually this is Tom Thumb) or is snatched from home by a creature (as is usually the case with Thumbelina, when a toad decides the tiny girl would be a perfect bride for her son). The child endures many challenges—Tom Thumb is nearly eaten by various animals, and Thumbelina is expected to marry a mole after she escapes the toad family with the help of a butterfly. Each uses wits, bravery, and the kindness of others to ultimately find security and happiness. For Thumbelina, this means she is crowned Queen of the Flower People and rules them beside her tiny king. Depending on the variant, Tom Thumb is either joyfully reunited with his parents or triumphantly knighted, after many harrowing escapes.

Versions and Variants to Consider

All over the world, there are variant stories about a tiny child born to parents who desperately want a baby. Often the child is a boy, but occasionally she is a girl, as with Hans Christian Andersen's *Thumbelina*. The overlap of some of the themes of "Thumbelina" and "Tom Thumb" (and story variants with male *and* female heroes!) make them interesting choices for the early childhood classroom. In addition, young children are fascinated by stories of tiny people who overcome great odds and identify with these mighty heroes!

Thumbelina, retold and illustrated by Caldecott Honor winner Brian Pinkney, is particularly appropriate for younger preschoolers. While true to Andersen's story, Pinkney leaves out many of the descriptions, making for a shorter, tighter text. Large, vibrant illustrations depicting Thumbelina and all of the human (and fairy) characters as Black make this perfect for circle time.

Thumbelina, retold by Amy Ehrlich and illustrated by Susan Jeffers, has detailed pictures and many full scenes from the natural world Thumbelina lives in.

Thumbelina, retold by Lauren Mills, adds to the original story, relating how Thumbelina's elderly mother is worried that no one will look after her daughter when she dies and asks a kind witch for advice. The witch tells her that she will know when it's time for Thumbelina to learn to fend for herself. When the mother notices her daughter gazing out of the window, longing to see the outside world, the mother decides it's time and leaves the window open, which is how the toad finds the young girl.

There are two main versions of "Tom Thumb" in picture book form. One comes from the Brothers Grimm, and the other has roots in King Arthur's realm and includes the wizard Merlin, who brings the tiny boy to yearning parents. In the Grimms' version, Tom yearns for adventure and plays tricks on bad guys, while in the Arthurian variant Tom defeats a giant. In both versions, Tom is swallowed by a cow and faces other perils because of his size.

Tom Thumb, by Eric Blair, is a short retelling with cartoonlike illustrations cast in modern times. It is a good way to introduce younger children to the basic Grimms' story.

Tom Thumb, by Eric Carle, is actually a short collection of stories from the Brothers Grimm that includes Tom Thumb. The story is faithful to the Grimms' telling, and Carle's characteristic style will excite young *The Very Hungry Caterpillar* fans.

Tom Thumb, retold and illustrated by Richard Jesse Watson, starts with a disguised Merlin's visit to the home of a poor farmer and his wife and ends with Tom being knighted by King Arthur himself and returning home to his delighted parents. The large, detailed illustrations are well-suited to group sharing, and the story is written in a relaxed and accessible way.

Most of the versions available in picture book format are retellings of the European tales, although the Japanese variant, "Issun Boshi," is available in some libraries. Delve more deeply into the story with master storyteller Margaret Read MacDonald's *Tom Thumb*, which includes many easy-to-tell variants of the tale from around the globe. Children fascinated by the adventures of truly small characters may appreciate the variety of stories, even without pictures!

Themes of Attachment and Relationships

In most variants of "Tom Thumb" and "Thumbelina," the parents desperately want a baby, and they love and protect the child even though Tom Thumb/Thumbelina is quite different from the infant they had wished for. What an affirming thought for children! However, even though the parents love the child, they cannot keep them safe. This can resonate deeply with children who are experiencing challenges—if their parents cannot make them feel secure, it is not because they do not love them.

As in other fairy tales, Tom Thumb/Thumbelina is helped along the way by animals who act as older, wiser supports. While we might not think of birds or butterflies or mice as competent adults, they play the same role in this fairy tale as the (adult) magical helpers in other fairy tales. They offer children hope that when the going gets tough, friendly faces will appear to help.

Questions to Explore the Protective Factor of Attachment with Children

1. What are some ways Tom Thumb's and Thumbelina's parents showed them that they loved them?

2. How do you think Thumbelina's mother felt when she discovered she was gone?

3. Who were the helpers in "Thumbelina"? Who were the helpers in "Tom Thumb"?

4. How do you think Tom/Thumbelina felt when they got help?

Themes of Initiative and Executive Functions

It is easy to see Tom Thumb's initiative. He is an adventurous boy who wants to do and see things for himself despite his size and the challenges it presents. He even uses his small size to get out of tough situations and solve problems. He is not only brave but quick-witted and resourceful.

Thumbelina demonstrates both self-efficacy and problem solving as well. After fish and a butterfly help her escape from the toads, the story mentions how she lived by herself at the edge of a stream. While not much detail is given, she makes herself a bed and finds food and drink in the wild for the whole summer. She also seeks a new shelter once the snows begin to fall.

In addition, when forced to choose between marrying the mole and spending her life in darkness or running into the unknown and being free, she chooses freedom. Although she initially refuses the swallow's offer to take her away from the mole because she doesn't want to upset a field mouse who has been kind to her, at the last minute she honors her own feelings and flies away with her friend. While young children will not understand the adult undertones of this decision, all have been told to do something they don't want to do or asked to play with someone they don't want to play with. While we encourage everyone to "be friends," it's important for children to know that if something feels uncomfortable, they have the right to express this.

Questions to Explore the Protective Factor of Initiative with Children

1. How do you think Tom Thumb felt when his father agreed to let him do things by himself (for example, bring the cart, go off with the men in exchange for gold, go after the giant)?

2. How do you think Thumbelina felt when she found herself all alone after her friend the butterfly rescued her? What did she do to take care of herself?

3. Why do you think Thumbelina got on the swallow's back instead of marrying the mole like the field mouse wanted her to? [Note: This may resonate with children who have experienced abuse, especially sexual abuse. If they begin to share things in a group setting that you feel are more appropriate for one-to-one conversation, it's fine to redirect the discussion with something like "That must have been scary for you. Let's talk about ways you were/could be brave like Thumbelina when we look at the book together later." It is very important not to add to the child's shame or negative feelings by either ignoring the comment or expressing shock or displeasure (but follow up as required).]

Themes of Self-Regulation

Both Tom Thumb and Thumbelina have moments of self-regulation. When they are scared, they don't freeze—they act. When Tom falls asleep in the hay on his adventures, he gets swallowed by a cow. In several variants he picks up a piece of the hay to tickle the cow's belly until she coughs him out. He also is very quiet when he is hiding.

While Thumbelina initially weeps and wails when things get tough, she rises to the occasion and overcomes her fear enough to ask for help. She also calms herself when she encounters the injured bird, which is much bigger than she is, and then repeatedly sneaks through the dark tunnel to take care of it. By the time she takes her final leap of faith on the back of the swallow, she climbs aboard confidently, quickly tying her sash around a feather so she will be secure.

Children know fear of the unknown. It may be walking into a new child care room or meeting a new pet—rather than being swallowed by a cow or riding on a giant bird's back—but their experiences are just as real. We must acknowledge and help them identify all their emotions, including fear, and support them in managing them in appropriate ways.

Questions to Explore the Protective Factor of Self-Regulation with Children

1. What is the scariest thing that happened to Tom Thumb/Thumbelina? What did they do when they were scared?

2. When have you been scared? What did you do?

Additions to the Story Center

This story inspires children to imagine tiny worlds. Stock your story center with all sorts of small supplies.

- Small papers, crayons, and books

- Sticky notes of various sizes

- Golf pencils or small pencils that come in packs for party favors

- "Books" for Thumbelina and Tom Thumb. Staple sticky notes inside small covers made of construction paper or pieces of children's fingerpaintings. Note: Many preschoolers do not have the fine-motor skills to draw tiny pictures or letters with tiny pencils. Expect even children who normally can make pictorial representations or recognizable letter forms to fill the tiny papers and books with "scribble writing." Ask them to read the miniature books to you (or to a doll/small figure representing Tom or Thumbelina), and record their stories on larger paper for use in a storytelling/storyacting circle.

Ideas for Storytelling/Storyacting

When tiny characters appear in children's stories, challenge children to make themselves a tiny boy or a huge bird during storyacting. This engages their imaginations in spatial reasoning. Similarly, animals that hop, swim, or fly in the stories offer wonderful opportunities to stretch children's movement vocabularies as they internalize the meanings of action words with their bodies.

Many children's stories involve being gobbled up by animals. In the storyacting process, encourage children playing the eaters to show how they look eating. The children being eaten can show what it might feel like to be in someone's tummy. (Young children don't have the biological knowledge to be concerned about being digested and what happens next.)

Flowers play a large role in "Thumbelina." Inviting children to be flowers in storyacting includes children who feel timid: few will refuse to be a flower or a tree. Encourage children to think of what flowers look like tightly budded and then blooming as they act out these parts of the story.

Caring Magic
Big Me, Little Me Body Tracings

Tracing children's bodies on large paper is a common preschool activity. This variation increases the fun and learning by adding a miniature tracing to go along with the story and stimulate more thinking about size.

You will need:

- A piece of bulletin board paper for each child, large enough to trace their body
- A piece of 12" x 18" construction paper for each child
- Dolls
- Pencils or crayons for tracing (so children do not get marker on dolls)

1. Ask each child to lie down on their large piece of paper. They may wish to get in an action pose.

2. Carefully trace around their bodies, describing what you are doing: "I'm tracing up your long, strong arm now! Here I go, around your head with all those smart brains inside!"

3. When you have finished, ask the children to color or paint their clothes, draw their faces and hair, and so on. Wait to cut out the figures until they have been decorated.

4. Ask the children to trace the Tom Thumb or Thumbelina version of themselves, using dolls on the construction paper. Assist younger children and those with less developed fine-motor skills by holding down the paper with masking tape.

5. After completing the doll tracing, encourage the children to color or paint their "mini me" to either match or contrast their own body tracing. Many preschoolers will need help cutting out around these smaller figures. Note: Older children may be able to do these smaller tracings while their friends are being traced. Younger children will benefit from being traced first to get experience with the entire process, scaffolded with the teacher's descriptions of what they are doing.

6. Hang up the tracings to create displays.
   - Make one display with the "giant" children and another with the tiny children. The children can draw, paint, or construct other images from the stories (for example, trees, flowers, mice, toads, animals) to decorate.
   - Make a display with both the giant and the tiny children.
   - If children tell/dictate stories about their characters, transcribe and add to the display.

How it builds attachment and relationships

The "Tom Thumb" and "Thumbelina" fairy tales inspire children to wonder about what it would be like to be tiny—or huge. This activity gives them the chance to be both and so supports their ability to decenter, or consider things from another perspective. It is also a collaborative activity between teacher and child. There is a physical and emotional closeness in the act of carefully tracing around a child, and this one-on-one attention is an opportunity to build trust. It also lets busy teachers really focus on each individual child. Just as the parents in these stories yearned for a child, young children generally adore their teachers and caregivers, and quiet shared moments like these affirm these relationships.

Co-creating a large-as-life mural with their classmates also offers children a chance to experience being part of the group. They can clearly see that they are part of this colorful group of friends, both large and small!

Finger Puppets

Stories about children "no bigger than a thumb" are a natural lead-in to making simple finger puppets with children.

You will need:

- Materials for the puppet base that the children will have the easiest time manipulating (for example, the fingers of rubber or cotton gloves, chenille stems wrapped around a finger, simple paper cones that can slide over a finger, commercially made finger puppets [optional])

- Art materials to decorate puppets

1. Lay out your choice of puppet-base materials or allow children to choose from a selection. Demonstrate how each can come to life by putting them on your own finger and talking. Have children do the same.

2. Help the children add faces to their finger puppets (drawn on paper or stickers, cut from magazines or photographs of children, or constructed from craft supplies, depending on the fine-motor skills of the children). Young children find puppets magical even if they are just a cone of paper with googly eyes!

3. After children have their puppets, invite them to name, describe, and talk to them and then tell their stories. These may be related to Tom Thumb/ Thumbelina or go in a completely different direction.

How it builds attachment and relationships

Children learn a great deal about relationships by acting out what they have seen and heard. Just as they model relationships when they play with dolls or other figures in dramatic play, they take on roles with puppets. Having complete control over both sides of a conversation, as when they talk with their puppet or hold a puppet on each hand, allows them to experiment and make sense out of the interactions that surround them. Listening to these interactions gives us insight into how they perceive their experiences.

When children enter puppet play together, each has to maintain a role of the puppet and often play a separate character themselves. If one child is Mother, and her puppet is Thumbelina, and the other is Father, and his puppet is Tom Thumb, the children have to juggle various perspectives while also paying attention to what their friend is saying. These relationship skills, like those in other kinds of pretend play, are invaluable as children navigate how to establish and maintain relationships.

Doing Magic: Playing Magic

Props for Dramatic Play

- Wings (either store-bought costume wings or fabric to flap as children imagine being birds or fairies)
- Stuffed animals representing cows, toads, mice, or birds
- Small baby dolls and miniature child dolls
- Fabric scraps for making beds, clothes, and so on
- Flowers (silk or plastic)
- Teacups

Props for Blocks/Building and STEM

- Farm animals
- Wagons
- People figures (small)
- Cylinders and flags for castle building (if King Arthur variants of "Tom Thumb" are read)

Props for the Discovery/Science Center

- Grasses
- Straw or hay
- Walnut shells and other nut shells (if there are no allergies in the room)
- Bird feathers
- Magnifying glasses
- Tiny objects (playing pieces from board games, miniature "favors" from party stores, and so on)

Props for Sensory Tables

- Water table: Boats created in Loose-Part Boat Making (see below); leaves or lily pads (real or plastic); small figures; plastic fish, toads, or frogs; rocks
- Fill sensory table with straw, if available, and hide small objects.
- Use sensory table to showcase individual small worlds (see page 108), or have children collaboratively build small worlds.

Doing Magic: Making Magic
Loose-Part Boat Making

Leaves or tiny boats carry the heroes in many versions. Constructing boats is a great STEM opportunity that invites sink/float experiments in your sensory table.

You will need:

- A variety of natural materials as well as things that can be used to attach the materials together (for suggestions see the list in appendix A)
- Material for sails, such as colored paper or leaves
- Baskets or pie tins (optional)
- Small people figures or plastic animals
- Sensory table or a bucket or basin

1. Show children pictures of boats in Thumbelina/Tom Thumb books. Discuss the pros and cons of various materials or allow children to dig right in.

2. Organize materials in baskets, pie tins, or piles, and allow children to experiment with their choice of materials to construct a boat. Not all boats will look like boats. Children are most productive when they can experiment without worrying about appearances. Small people figures or plastic animals may also inspire the builders.

3. Provide a sensory table with water or a bucket or basin for children to try out their boats. If boats sink, discuss ideas to improve children's designs.

4. Allow children to modify their designs if they choose.

How it builds initiative and executive functions

Construction of all kinds supports problem solving, which is part of initiative. When children have a specific task, they need to draw on past knowledge, including what they remember from the story and what they know about boats. Young children use cognitive flexibility as they handle materials to explore possibilities: If I want these sticks to stay together like a raft, I could use glue or playdough or tape or a rubber band. Which will work better?

Because children have the story for inspiration and the opportunity to try out their boats in water, they have a strong motivation to persevere and succeed, another aspect of initiative. Given a choice of materials, their self-efficacy blossoms.

Small World Maker Space

In their books *StoryMaking* and *Makerspaces*, Michelle Compton and Robin Thompson (2018, 2020) describe how providing children with a changing variety of open-ended materials in sensory stations extends the soothing play in these centers into creative problem solving and literacy opportunities as children create small worlds. Thumbelina/Tom Thumb stories lend themselves naturally to creating and exploring small worlds.

You will need:

- Sensory table or individual tubs, baskets, bins, or aluminum baking dishes, depending on whether children will be working individually or collaboratively

- A variety of natural materials (for suggestions see the list in appendix A). Younger children may do better with fewer choices as they get started.

- Clear, blue, green, or brown flat glass "pebbles" (available at party supply stores and used to fill vases) for water

- Base material such as green or brown playdough that objects stick into easily and that can be molded into hills, valleys, and so forth. Note: Have children help make playdough from an online recipe to offer them an additional learning opportunity that targets math, science, fine-motor, language, and social skills.

- An "idea jar" with a variety of small figures of people and animals, collected from other centers in your classroom

1. Offer the children the materials and provide scaffolding only if needed. (The goal of the maker movement is for children to explore, experiment, imagine, and represent, rather than copy and conform.) If children have ideas for using other materials, facilitate this as well.

2. After children have constructed a small world, encourage them to choose a figure to add to it.

3. Leave time for children to play in their small world and share what they created. If many children are involved, Compton and Thompson (2020) suggest children share with a partner so everyone has a chance to share and no one has to sit listening for an extended period of time.

How it builds initiative and executive functions

Like the boat-building activity, creating a small world offers many opportunities for problem solving, persistence, and creative representation. Seeing one's own ideas come to fruition is a powerful feeling for anyone, and young children

especially find this rewarding. Promote children's awareness of their own initiative by posing questions during the process. For example, when the children first examine the materials, you might say, "What kind of home could you imagine making for Tom Thumb or Thumbelina from these materials?" or "Think about the adventures that Tom Thumb and Thumbelina went on. I wonder if you could use these materials to create one of the places they explored?" This puts the making soundly under the children's control so they can take ownership for their ideas, their problem solving, and their ability to complete a creation.

While it's important not to interrupt a child's concentration, asking questions during the making can also promote initiative. A simple "Tell me about this hump here" invites children to articulate their thinking and affirms that you are interested and engaged in their problem solving. Avoid closed-ended yes/no questions like "Is that hump a mountain?" This cues children that you aren't sure what their creation is, undermining confidence and self-efficacy.

Offer descriptions rather than value judgments: "I see you've stuck a lot of twigs in the playdough so they can stand up" tells the child you recognize their ideas and hard work. In contrast, "I like how you put in all these trees!" puts the focus on your own feelings about the child's work rather than their feelings about it. Children want to please us, but this does not necessarily enhance their confidence in taking creative risks. After being immersed in stories about how tiny children can be brave, be resourceful, and overcome all odds, we want children to see themselves as just as brave and resourceful, even if the world they control is in a pie pan and made of playdough!

Superpower Magic
Each Peach Pear Plum, I Spy Tom Thumb!

The rhyming I spy book *Each Peach Pear Plum* by Janet and Allan Ahlberg features many fairy tale and nursery rhyme characters. The first page starts with "Each Peach Pear Plumb, I spy Tom Thumb."

You will need:

- Small Tom Thumb figure, such as a Lego person, action figure, small doll, or wooden character from the block area

1. After reading the book, play "I spy Tom Thumb." Ask the children to cover their eyes while you (or a child) hide a small Tom Thumb figure. The figure should be at least partly in plain sight from where the children are sitting.

2. Ask the children to use only their eyes to scan the room. When a child sees Tom, they say, "Each Peach Pear Plum, I spy Tom Thumb!"

3. Have the child tiptoe over to Tom and point at him. They may then hide Tom for the next round, if desired.

4. Repeat activity as long as interest and time warrant.

How it builds self-regulation

Every step of this process encourages children to self-regulate. We know it's hard for children to keep their eyes closed or covered, so be sure that Tom is hidden quickly if children still are in the "peeking" stage. Scanning the room to find the figure supports children's focus, concentration, and working memory. The child who first spots Tom Thumb will be tempted to leap up and run to grab him, so shouting the rhyme encourages them to control their first impulse. Older children can do the hiding, and this challenges them, as it is hard not to blurt out clues to their friends.

Transition Activity: Naptime Horse Whisperer

In many versions of "Tom Thumb," Tom sits in a horse's ear so he can quietly guide the horse and cart to find his father in the forest. Because he is whispering, the passersby wonder how the horse and cart can travel without a driver.

- Choose a child to be Tom Thumb. Ask the child to quietly tiptoe to each "horse" and whisper that it's time to find a cot for naptime. The horses quietly *clip-clop* to their naptime space. Adapt this for your own nap-time routine or use for other transition times (line up, go wash hands, and so on).

- Consider choosing children for whom self-regulation is a challenge; the responsibility of having this job, combined with the rich imagery from the story, may help them self-regulate more than usual.

Transition Activity: Follow the Swallow

In "Thumbelina," the swallow helps Thumbelina escape from the mole.

- As you start a transition from one place to another, remind the children how gently the bird must have flown so Thumbelina would not fall off.

- With a feather (or a pretend feather), lightly touch each child to turn them into swallows.

- Lead them slowly and gracefully to their destination, gently flapping your wings.

Three Billy Goats Gruff:
The Magic of Standing Up for Yourself

Story Magic

There are three billy goats named Gruff. They live on a rocky hillside and want to go to the grassy hillside across the river so they can eat and grow fat. Unfortunately, a troll lives under the bridge they have to cross. The smallest billy goat goes first, *trip trap trip trap.* The troll says he's going to eat him. The smallest goat says to wait for his bigger brother, who is much bigger and will make a better meal. The troll agrees. The middle-sized billy goat goes next, *Trip Trap Trip Trap.* The troll pops up and says he's going to eat him. The middle-sized billy goat says to wait for his bigger brother. The troll agrees. The biggest billy goat crosses the bridge: *TRIP TRAP TRIP TRAP.* The troll says he is going to eat him. The biggest billy goat says to try. When the troll does, the biggest billy goat butts him into the water and the troll is never seen again. The three billy goats gruff eat the grass on the other side of the river and are probably still there. We finish with a flourish: "Snip Snap Snout! This tale's told out!" (a traditional Norwegian ending to storytelling).

Versions and Variants to Consider

This simple, rhythmic folktale has enthralled children for generations and may be more accessible for the youngest children than some of the more complex popular fairy tales. Many, many versions are available: bilingual (including American Sign Language), lift-a-flap, pop-up, and ones told from the troll's point of view. Most are based on the original Norwegian tale.

The Three Billy Goats Gruff, written by Paul Galdone, features bright, clear pictures. The size makes it well-suited for group story times. Galdone is a master at using the goats' eyes to express their emotions.

The Three Billy Goats Gruff, written by Marcia Brown, sticks to the original Norwegian version, including a description of the biggest billy goat poking out the troll's eyes with his horns and crushing "him to bits, body and bones." Most children will applaud the mean troll getting what's coming, but, as with all books, make sure to read it all the way through before sharing it.

The Three Billy Goats Gruff, written by Glen Rounds, has a distinctive style with childlike and clear illustrations. He uses font size to differentiate the characters' voices, which children who have started to make sense of print may notice.

The Three Billy Goats Gruff, written by Jerry Pinkney, won a Caldecott Medal for its detailed and realistic illustrations. Pinkney takes some liberties with the story: there are more descriptions and the ending has a twist—the bully troll gets a taste of his own medicine when a larger fish threatens to eat the troll in the river. But the last page shows the troll building a hut, suggesting he might be getting a fresh start.

Themes of Attachment and Relationships

Siblings and peers are often important sources of support for young children, even when adults don't always live up to expectations. Unlike many fairy tales that highlight competition between brothers and sisters, "The Three Billy Goats Gruff" offers the message that someone always has your back and together you can stand up to bullies. Children see that the brothers are a team and take care of themselves and each other.

Questions to Explore the Protective Factor of Attachment with Children

1. Can you think of a time when your sibling or good friend helped you? How did you feel?

2. Can you think of a time when you helped a sibling or friend? How did you feel?

Themes of Initiative and Executive Functions

This simple story highlights the protective factor of initiative in all its forms. First, the billy goats show self-efficacy when they want to get to the grassy hillside, and even the littlest one is confident he will make it. Motivation to succeed is demonstrated when they each persevere: no troll is going to stop them. They also use their wits and problem solve around the troll's challenge: by appealing to his greedy self, the first two billy goats trick him into letting them pass.

For young children, it is a quintessential story about overcoming fear of the troll, a bully. Helping them to frame the story in this way invites them to reflect on their own fears and consider ways they too persevere in the face of obstacles.

Questions to Explore the Protective Factor of Initiative with Children

1. Which billy goat do you think was the bravest? Why?

2. Can you think of a time when you did something brave? What did you feel like before you did it? How did you feel afterward?

Themes of Self-Regulation

Connected to the billy goats' initiative is their ability to self-regulate. How many of us would jump out of our skins if we were trip-trapping across a bridge and a huge monster popped up? While a few variants mention the smallest billy goat trembling, most give us very little indication of what the goats are feeling. Instead, we see a calm, quick-witted response to the troll: a perfect example of billy goat self-regulation.

Because the text is so sparse, it is easy to add in calming strategies you use in your classroom. This is especially effective as the children act out the story. For example, if you have children take three deep breaths as a strategy to slow themselves down, suggest the billy goats do this before they head across the bridge or after the troll jumps up.

Questions to Explore the Protective Factor of Self-Regulation with Children

1. How do you think the smallest billy goat felt when he started across the bridge? What about the middle billy goat? The biggest billy goat?

2. What do you do if you feel a little bit scared or nervous?

3. Who can you ask for help?

Additions to the Story Center

To freshen your story center for the "The Three Billy Goats Gruff," think about the three sizes of the billy goats and add:

- Three sizes of writing utensils in three separate containers: thick markers, thin markers, and crayons; or colored pencils, crayons, and short, thick toddler crayons or broken crayon stubs

- Three sizes of paper, staplers, paper clips, and sticky notes

- As many colors of green crayons and/or markers as you can find to represent the grass that tempted the billy goats

Ideas for Storytelling/Storyacting

Children may pick up on the repetition in the story and use it as a model. The troll often shows up, offering a good chance to support children's self-regulation during encounters with other characters. For example, you might say, "How can the billy goat push the troll into the water without touching him? Remember, we don't touch each other in story circle." The "*trip traps*" give children an example of onomatopoeia (using words that resemble actual sounds) to use in their stories.

This is also an outstanding story to use in storyacting as is. It is short enough to retell from memory, or use a one-page summary (readily available online) to read the story without having to turn pages. Whether children have lots of experience with storyacting or are new to the process, this story offers lots of action to engage even timid story actors. There is also a bridge—usually best with two children—as well as the grassy hillside ("How could you make your body like a hillside?").

Caring Magic
Class Billy Goat Mural

The whole class works together in this activity to grow a grassy hillside and flowing creek, complete with billy goats and the troll, using repurposed finger-paintings and torn paper. What a great way to brighten a wall—and the spirit of teamwork!

You will need:

- A large piece of bulletin board or butcher paper
- Children's fingerpaintings in brown, blue, and green, torn or cut up, repurposed from other projects or created in advance
- Construction paper strips and construction paper "snips" (see Sensory Table suggestion on page 119)
- Three-dimensional objects like sticks, rope, craft sticks, and so on
- Googly eyes, chenille stems, yarn, cotton balls
- Construction paper
- Glue and other adhesives, duct tape, and staplers

1. Invite some children to create the background scenery for the mural, using the torn-up fingerpaintings and construction paper bits to make rocky and grassy hillsides, water, and so on. Sketch a rough outline of the two hillsides with a place for the stream to flow in between so the children will have an idea of where to attach their torn paper.

2. Have other children look at the bridges in several versions of the story. Ask "How can we make a bridge for our mural?"

3. As some children work on billy goats and the troll, others can problem solve how to construct the bridge to the scale of the mural. Provide sticks, string, rope, and other loose parts to inspire their thinking about bridges. Encourage them to try out their ideas by laying them out on the mural first, and then, when they are satisfied, attaching the parts.

4. Make a billy goat by tearing a rectangle of paper. Suggested sizes: 12" x 18" for the biggest billy goat; 9" x 12" for the middle-sized billy goat; and 4.5" x 6" (half of 9" x 12") for the smallest billy goat.

5. No matter what size paper you are using, start by folding it in half (like a "hamburger," not a "hot dog"). Most preschoolers will have a tough time with the folding, so you may want to do this yourself. Then have children tear (not cut) along the fold.

6. Fold one of the two pieces in half (hamburger-style) again; children will tear along this fold as well. There will now be three pieces (one bigger, two smaller) for each goat.

7. Have the children tear around the perimeter of the largest rectangle; this becomes the body.

8. Ask the children to tear one of the smaller pieces into an oval for the head. Lightly draw an oval on the paper to guide younger children's tearing. Then ask the children to tear the other smaller piece into four legs.

9. Depending on how the children tear out the head piece, there may be rounded "edge" pieces to make the billy goat's horns. If not, tear horns from other scraps of paper or fashion from chenille stems and staple onto the head.

10. After all pieces are torn, ask the children to attach them to the mural with tape, glue, or staples and add eyes, beards, tails, and other features. The troll can be constructed in the same way (tearing out the body, head, arms, and legs) or be drawn or painted.

11. Allow children to make more billy goats and trolls if they'd like to. In several versions, there are multiple goats who find their way to the grassy slope after the first three get there. And maybe the troll has a family or friends lurking beneath the bridge!

How it builds attachment and relationships

Constructing a mural with teachers and classmates over several days offers children many opportunities for relationship building. Young children often see their artistic creations as individual efforts. Collaborating on a big project is a terrific way to feel you are an important member of the classroom. Even younger children or those with less developed fine-motor skills can contribute. Using finger-painting (the most process-oriented of the process arts) to make the background and having children tear the paper instead of cutting with scissors ensures that all children can join in. The natural sharing of ideas and excitement of making a large and story-connected mural affirms friendships and builds trust among all children. The mural's ongoing presence in the classroom subtly reminds children of this.

Puppet Play

This is an excellent story for children to re-create—and extend—with puppets because of its simplicity. Flannel boards and magnet boards with the billy goats and troll offer the same benefits of retelling the story. However, puppets seem to invite children to go "off-script" more readily, and this allows them to explore the relationships between the characters of the story.

You will need:

- Puppets of the three billy goats and the troll (purchased or made by the children)
  - Paper bag puppets are easy to make from lunch bags; children can draw on faces or use patterns available online.
  - Puppets can even be made with chenille stems wrapped around the finger. A pom-pom for the head is held in place by twisting the ends around it, which form billy goat horns.
- A puppet stage is optional and not recommended unless the children show that they are ready to extend the puppet play over multiple days. In this case, identifying a table in the classroom as "the bridge" can add to the play.

1. Keep it child directed! After children have heard several versions of the story, place a basket with the puppets in the library center.

How it builds attachment and relationships

Whether children are interacting with each other or playing by themselves with one puppet on each hand, playing with puppets develops social-emotional skills. This story highlights the positive relationship between the brothers as well as the conflict between the billy goats and the troll. Children acting out scenarios with these characters explore both kinds of relationships.

We work hard with children to avoid conflict, but it is inevitable. Many teachers share social problem-solving strategies, such as (1) identify the problem, (2) generate solutions, (3) pick a solution, and (4) try it out. When children use these in pretend play, they gain mastery over them. Using puppets adds an extra layer of control. They are not resolving a conflict with a real person; it's a billy goat and a troll trying to figure things out!

Doing Magic: Playing Magic
Props for Blocks/Building and STEM

- Goat figures (If you don't have goats, print pictures found online and tape them to small blocks or toilet paper tubes.)
- Troll
- Lincoln Logs
- Craft sticks
- Pictures of different bridges

Props for Outside Play or Gross-Motor Areas

- Balance beams
- Bridges (Many centers have older wooden structures that flip from "bridge" to "row boat." This is the ideal time to haul it out of the closet!)

Props for Sensory Tables

- Water table: Foam blocks or small plastic bricks for bridges; plastic goats or other animals or people
- Sensory bins: Dirt or grass seed, plastic "Easter" grass, or crunched-up brown paper bags; craft sticks and playdough for bridge construction; small animals, if desired

- Snipping table: Turn a sensory table or bin into a snipping table, in honor of the story's ending: "Snip Snap Snout! This tale's told out!"
  - Place scraps of paper left over from art projects, pages from old newspapers and magazines, old stationery, and so on into the table, along with several pairs of scissors.
  - Snipping is the next developmental stage after tearing and is satisfying while building finger strength and coordination.
  - Snips can be recycled for other art projects, such as gluing to the mural or making collages.

Doing Magic: Making Magic
Class Billy Goat Mural

Creating the classroom billy goat mural (described in the Caring Magic section on page 115) not only offers children many opportunities for developing relationships and relationship skills but also promotes initiative in several ways.

How it builds initiative and executive functions

Children use their problem-solving skills as they decide how to arrange the rocky hillside and the grassy hillside as well as construct the bridge. Young children also develop self-efficacy. In fingerpainting, children take full control of their art exploration and making. Even children who are not yet able to draw anything recognizable can fill a paper with bold fingerpaint colors and movements to help create a mural of a beloved story and share their art-making meaningfully with friends, teachers, and family.

Tearing paper also promotes a child's sense of mastery. Because cutting is seen as an essential skill for kindergarten, we sometimes expect young children to practice this skill before they are ready, using "safety" scissors that are not sharp enough to efficiently cut paper. This sets up children for frustration and failure. With tearing, they can create art as they develop the pincer grasp and learn to work their hands in opposite directions, which will serve them well as they progress toward cutting and writing.

Creating the mural also contributes to children's motivation to succeed. So many projects done in our classrooms fit neatly into twenty-minute time blocks. A project that extends over multiple days shows children how much work goes into creating something big and complex and encourages them to persist in steadily moving toward a goal.

Bridge STEM Challenges

What if the billy goats decided to build another bridge, so they wouldn't have to deal with the troll? How could they do this?

You will need:

- Loose parts and natural materials suitable for bridge construction (for suggestions see the list in appendix A)
- Blue construction paper or felt squares (for the river that their bridge must go across)
- Picture of a billy goat taped to a small wooden unit block

1. Invite children to explore the materials: What are they like? What are some ways to build with them?

2. Ask them to construct a bridge for the billy goats to cross. The bridge should be long enough to cross over the paper or felt river and strong enough to support the weight of the block billy goat.

3. After construction is finished, invite the builders to share their work. Consider taking pictures of their constructions to add to your block area.

How it builds initiative and executive functions

Like other STEM challenges, this activity stimulates problem solving, executive function skills, and what Eleanor Duckworth called "the having of wonderful ideas" (2006). Loose parts encourage cognitive flexibility. Children are fascinated by what objects can do, and seeing a toilet paper roll as a support for a bridge, or as the bridge itself, pushes them to examine objects' attributes in new ways. Working memory kicks in after they come up with a great idea: instead of getting distracted by rolling the tubes around for fun, they may methodically begin to balance loose parts on the tube supports to determine which will create a strong and billy goat–worthy bridge.

As anyone who has ever used loose parts knows, things don't always work the way you anticipated. It seems like a chenille stem placed across two cardboard tubes should be a bridge—it looks like a bridge—but the billy goat knocks down the whole thing! Regulating emotions and focusing on fixing the problem rather than giving up in frustration are important benefits of this activity for children. Both peers and adults can scaffold these situations and offer questions that help the child find solutions that work better.

Superpower Magic
Walking the Bridge

With or without a prop, children love to pretend to walk across high places. The story connection adds to the fun and self-regulation in this activity.

> You will need:

- Masking or duct tape (alternatively, use a balance beam instead of tape for an added challenge)

1. Place the tape "bridge" on the floor. Adjust the width to meet children's gross-motor needs and adjust the length depending on experience and age of the children.

2. Have the children take turns carefully walking over the bridge.

3. If a child "falls off" into the water (the floor or carpet), "dry off" the child and then ask the child to return to the line.

4. Continue until interest wanes. Add a challenge by having children say, "Trip trap," as they are crossing, walking across on tippy toes (to be extra quiet so as not to wake the troll), or even walking backward.

How it builds self-regulation

We often think of self-regulation in terms of children managing behaviors and emotions, such as shoving other children, continuing to play when asked to clean up, and having angry outbursts or tantrums. However, these are just the symptoms of self-regulation challenges. Self-regulation starts with regulating one's movement and actions. Research shows that today's preschoolers often have a harder time doing this than previous generations, in part because they have fewer opportunities for focused movement activities (Bodrova, Germeroth, and Leong 2013).

This simple activity asks children to practice their focus and concentration as they control their bodies. It improves their physical coordination, but the bigger benefit is inside their brains. By framing the activity within the story they know, they draw on the extraordinary power of their imaginations to support their developing self-regulation skills.

Red Light, Green Light—Troll Style

This is the familiar childhood game, with a slight twist: The person who calls, "Red light, green light," is now a troll, and the area the children cross is the bridge. No materials are needed, though chalk or tape to mark start and stop points is optional.

1. Make sure children know about stoplights (children in rural areas may not) and that green means go and red means stop.

2. Assign one child to be the troll, and have them stand at one end of the play space while the other children (the billy goats) stand at the other.

3. Have the troll turn their back to the billy goats and call, "Green light!" Ask the billy goats to move toward the troll across the "bridge."

4. Have the troll call, "Red light!" and spin around, at which point the billy goats must freeze. If the troll sees someone still moving, they return to the start. The first billy goat that reaches the troll gets to be the troll for the next round.

How it builds self-regulation

Red Light, Green Light builds self-regulation skills for both the billy goats and the troll. The "troll" has to listen to the movement of children they can't see and remember to say, "Red light!" before turning around. The billy goats have to listen attentively for the call of "Red light!" or "Green light!" and act on it immediately. We know how hard it is for young children to stop something that they are enjoying (like sneaking up to the troll!).

Children's need for repeated practice in this kind of self-regulatory activity may well be why so many traditional games offer similar opportunities. Children's games in the past were often unregulated by adults (that is, self-regulated), and the ones that were played repeatedly, adapted, and passed on to friends provided just the right level of challenge, peril, and fun. Playing such games for hours was not uncommon, and it may be that the lack of time and opportunity to engage in this kind of play is another contributing factor to the self-regulation challenges we see in so many children.

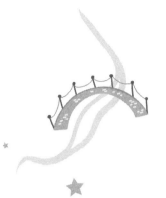

Transition Activity: Trip-Trap Transitions

Trip-trapping offers children the scaffolding they need to transition between locations in an orderly and playful way.

- For relatively quiet transitions, children can be the smallest billy goat and whisper, "Trip trap," as they tiptoe or move lightly to their destinations.

- When a bit more noise is permissible, they can be the middle-sized billy goat and say, "Trippety trap, trippety trap" in a normal voice.

- When it's okay to be loud, they can stomp and say, "TRIP TRAP," in their biggest billy goat voices.

- Note: Children will do better as the smallest, quietest billy goat if you give them opportunities to be the biggest and boldest billy goat too!

Transition Activity: Yoga Bridge Pose

This yoga pose can help children stretch out tired bodies and relax before nap or keep them engaged as they wait for their peers to arrive on the carpet. Before nap use a calm voice and emphasize stretching that hardworking back. If waiting for peers, consider encouraging children to see how high they can make their bridges to add a level of challenge.

- Have children lie on their backs with knees bent, feet together.

- Ask them to place their hands on their waists.

- Encourage children to try to raise their torsos, keeping elbows close to their bodies.

Online Material

Beauty and the Beast: The Magic of Being True to Yourself

Find a discussion of the beloved tale "Beauty and the Beast" and the accompanying ideas for how to use it to nurture resilience in young children online at www.redleafpress.org /her/bab.pdf.

Appendix A
Materials for Classroom Magic

Many of the projects and center suggestions in this book make use of easily gathered materials that invite children to make imaginative connections with the stories they are exploring. The specific materials offered are often less important than providing a wide variety of open-ended items for them to tinker, create, and take initiative with.

Asking families to help stock your loose-parts treasure chests is a wonderful way to involve them in their children's learning. Busy working parents may not ever be able to come in to share a snack or read a story, but most are willing to put empty toilet paper tubes and food boxes in a bag and send them in. Both families and children delight in contributing, and this builds relationships too!

Treasures from the Elves' Workshop: Examples of Repurposed Materials/Loose Parts	Treasures from Field and Forest: Examples of Natural Materials/Loose Parts
Cardboard tubes of various sizes	Rocks
Small boxes and cartons (for example, cereal boxes)	Pebbles
Milk cartons (rinsed)	Dirt (in bags/bowls)
Ribbon wheels	Sticks of various sizes
Spools	Twigs
Empty tape rolls	Bark
Used/outdated stationery	Wood "cookies"
Straws	Leaves
Corks	Pine cones
Buttons	Pine needles
Bottle caps	Acorns
	Walnut and other nut shells*

Treasures from the Elves' Workshop: Examples of Repurposed Materials/Loose Parts	Treasures from Field and Forest: Examples of Natural Materials/Loose Parts
Canning lids Marker lids Craft sticks Foil Keys Springs Nuts, bolts, washers, and so on Yarn String Twist ties Rubber bands Chenille stems (pipe cleaners) Cotton balls Net fruit bags Fabric remnants and scraps Old scarves Discarded jewelry Gems Beads	Seeds* Seedpods* Grasses Straw or hay Bird feathers Seashells Sea glass Flowers (real or fake) Moss or sphagnum moss Small gourds *Be aware of food allergies when choosing nuts and seeds. Examples of Attachments† Glue Paste Glue sticks Glue guns Tape Duct tape Masking tape Playdough Tacky putty Staplers Brads †Children use more problem-solving skills when allowed a choice of how they will stick together their creations.

Appendix B
Fairy Tale Variants

These fairy tale variants were referenced in this book. They represent a tiny tip of the magic wand that is the collection of fairy tales, both familiar and not so familiar, from every culture in the world. As you use fairy tales in your classroom, you will hopefully find many other favorites, as well as variants of other tales you think the children will enjoy.

Resilience is a universal trait, and the fairy tales from many lands offer a magic mirror into this powerful tool. As you select stories to share, it's important to be mindful that many tales were collected and retold when our understanding of cultural bias was not as well developed. Most are generally *not* appropriate for teaching young children about the specifics of different cultures. Instead, share them as a way of helping children to connect with that intricate web of Story that joins us together in resilience.

Before you read a book to children, be sure that you read it thoughtfully yourself. Are there stereotypes of cultures that can be discussed with children? Are there depictions of people or places that will mislead children or embarrass or hurt a child from that culture? We know, for the most part, that Europeans do not live in tiny cottages in the forest or magnificent palaces anymore. Similarly, the Indigenous peoples of the United States no longer typically live in tepees and wigwams. "Once upon a time" can set the stage for this by cueing children that they are entering the timeless land of Story, but be sure to stay alert to children's misunderstandings.

At the end of the list, you will find several resources to help you evaluate picture books of all kinds from an antibias perspective, as well as an article about choosing fairy tales for different ages.

Cinderella, or the Little Glass Slipper. 1955. Retold and illustrated by Marcia Brown. Scribner.

Cinderella. 2004. Retold by Amy Ehrlich, illustrated by Susan Jeffers. Dutton.

Yeh Shen: A Cinderella Story from China. 1982. Retold by Ai-Ling Louie, illustrated by Ed Young. Puffin.

The Golden Sandal: A Middle Eastern Cinderella Story. 1999. Retold by Rebecca Hickox, illustrated by Will Hillenbrand. Holiday House.

The Gift of the Crocodile: A Cinderella Story. 2000. Retold by Judy Sierra, illustrated by Reynold Ruffins. Simon & Schuster.

Chinye: A West African Folk Tale. 1994. Retold by Obi Onyefulu, illustrated by Evie Safarewicz. Viking Kestrel.

Little Gold Star/Estrellita de oro: A Cinderella Cuento Retold in Spanish and English. 2000. Retold by Joe Hayes, illustrated by Gloria Osuna Perez and Lucia Angela Perez. Cinco Puntos.

The Rough-Face Girl. 1992. Retold by Rafe Martin, illustrated by David Shannon. Putnam.

Ashpet: An Appalachian Tale. 1994. Retold by Joanne Compton, illustrated by Kenn Compton. Holiday House.

The Irish Cinderlad. 2000. Retold by Shirley Climo, illustrated by Loretta Krupinski. Trophy Picture Books.

Glass Slipper, Gold Sandal: A Worldwide Cinderella. 2007. Retold by Paul Fleishman, illustrated by Julie Paschkis. Henry Holt.

Hansel and Gretel. 1984. Retold by Rika Lesser, illustrated by Paul Zelinsky. Putnam and Grosset.

Hansel and Gretel. 1997. Retold and illustrated by Jane Ray. Candlewick.

Hansel and Gretel. 1990. Retold and illustrated by James Marshall. Dial Books.

Hansel and Gretel. 2001. Retold and illustrated by Beni Montresor. Atheneum.

Hansel and Gretel Stories around the World. 2017. Retold by Cari Meister, illustrated by multiple artists. Picture Window Books.

Rapunzel. 2008. Retold and illustrated by Rachel Isadora. Putnam.

Rapunzel. 1997. Retold and illustrated by Paul Zelinsky. Puffin Books.

Rapunzel. 2017. Retold by Chloe Perkins, illustrated by Archana Sreenivason. Simon and Schuster.

The Canary Prince. 1991. Retold and illustrated by Eric Jon Nones. Farrar, Straus and Giroux.

Jack and the Beanstalk. 1991. Retold and illustrated by Paul Galdone. Morrow Junior Books.

Jack and the Beanstalk. 1991. Retold and illustrated by Steven Kellogg. Morrow Junior Books.

Kate and the Beanstalk. 2005. Retold by Mary Pope Osborne, illustrated by Giselle Potter. Aladdin.

Jack and the Beanstalk. 2011. Retold and illustrated by Nina Crews. Henry Holt.

Thumbelina. 2003. Retold and illustrated by Brian Pinkney. Greenwillow Books.

Thumbelina. 2005. Retold by Amy Ehrlich, illustrated by Susan Jeffers. Dutton Juvenile.

Thumbelina. 2005. Retold and illustrated by Lauren Mills. Little, Brown.

Tom Thumb: A Retelling of the Grimms' Fairy Tale. 2011. Retold by Eric Blair, illustrated by Todd Irving Ouren. Picture Window Books.

Tom Thumb. 2011. Retold and illustrated by Eric Carle. Orchard Books.

Tom Thumb. 1993. Retold and illustrated by Richard Jesse Watson. HMH Books for Young Readers.

Tom Thumb. 1995. Retold by Margaret Read MacDonald. Oryx.

Each Peach Pear Plum. 1978. Written and illustrated by Janet and Allan Ahlberg. Scholastic.

The Three Billy Goats Gruff. 2001. Retold and illustrated by Paul Galdone. Clarion Books.

The Three Billy Goats Gruff. 1957. Retold and illustrated by Marcia Brown. Harcourt, Brace and World.

The Three Billy Goats Gruff. 1993. Retold and illustrated by Glen Rounds. Holiday House.

The Three Billy Goats Gruff. 2017. Retold and illustrated by Jerry Pinkney. Little, Brown.

Beauty and the Beast. 1985. Retold and illustrated by Warrick Hutton. Atheneum.

Beauties and Beasts. 1993. Collected and retold by Betsy Hearne. Oryx.

Beauty and the Beast. 1989. Retold and illustrated by Jan Brett. Clarion Books.

Beauty and the Beast. 2014. Retold by H. Chuku Lee, illustrated by Pat Cummings. Amistad.

Beauty and the Beast. 2017. Retold by Cynthia Rylant, illustrated by Meg Park. Hyperion.

The Great Smelly, Slobbery, Small-Tooth Dog. 2007. Retold by Margaret Read MacDonald, illustrated by Julie Paschkis. August House Little Folk.

The Dragon Prince. 1997. Retold by Laurence Yep, illustrated by Kam Mak. HarperCollins.

Teacher Resources for Selecting Stories

Derman-Sparks, Louise. 2013. "Guide for Selecting Anti-Bias Children's Books." Teaching for Change. https://socialjusticebooks.org/guide-for-selecting -anti-bias-childrens-books.

Seale, Doris, Beverly Slapin, and Rosemary Gonzales. 2000. How to Tell the Difference: A Guide for Evaluating Children's Books for Anti-Indian Bias. Oyate. www.oyate.org/index.php/resources/41-resources/how-to-tell-the -difference. (Although this is written about American Indians, it offers lots of food for thought when choosing books from any culture that is not your own.)

Almon, Joan. 2021. "Choosing Fairy Tales for Different Ages." http://waldorflibrary .org/articles/977-choosing-fairy-tales-for-different-ages.

Appendix C
Additional Resources

Other Children's Books Featuring Themes of Resilience

Because the protective factors for resilience are such "ordinary magic," many children's stories touch on them. Once you start looking, you'll discover that you can tweak the questions and match other books with favorite activities to nurture resilience throughout your curriculum.

Berger, Samantha. 2018. *What If…* New York: Little, Brown. (Cognitive Flexibility, Imagination)

Demi. 1990. *The Empty Pot*. New York: Henry Holt. (Self-Efficacy)

Jobb, Gigi. 2019. *A Whole Other Magic*. Edmonton, AB: Toadstool. (Relationships, Initiative, Play)

MacDonald, Margaret Read. 2018. *Tough Tug*. New York: Two Lions. (Self-Regulation, Mastery Motivation, Self-Efficacy)

Ringtved, Glenn. 2016. *Cry, Heart, but Never Break*. New York: Enchanted Lion Books. (Relationships, Emotions, Grief)

Rosenthal, Amy Drouse, and Tom Lichtenheld. 2009. *Duck! Rabbit!* San Francisco: Chronicle Books. (Peer Relationships, Taking Other Perspectives)

Seuss, Dr. 1996. *My Many-Colored Days*. New York: Knopf. (Identifying Emotions)

Waldman, Neil. 2013. *Al and Teddy*. Bronx, NY: Dream Yard Press. (Sibling Relationships, Imagination, Self-Regulation)

Yolen, Jane, and Chris Sheban. 2016. *What to Do with a Box*. Mankato, MN: Creative Editions. (Cognitive Flexibility)

Books and Websites to Further Your Journey

There are many books, articles, and websites that will help you to continue to create a treasure trove full of playful, creative, and resilience-focused experiences for the children in your care. Here are a few of my favorites!

Trauma

Erdman, Sarah, and Laura J. Colker. 2020. *Trauma & Young Children: Teaching Strategies to Support and Empower*. Washington, DC: National Association for the Education of Young Children.

Harris, Nadine Burk. 2018. *The Deepest Well: Healing the Long-Term Effects of Childhood Adversity*. Boston: Houghton Mifflin Harcourt.

Langworthy, Sara E. 2015. *Bridging the Relationship Gap: Connecting with Children Facing Adversity*. St. Paul, MN: Redleaf Press.

Statman-Weil, Katie. 2020. *Trauma-Responsive Strategies for Early Childhood*. St. Paul, MN: Redleaf Press.

Teaching for Resilience

Brooke, Jasmine. 2018. *Rapunzel, Let Down Your Zip Wire*. New York: Gareth Stevens.

Bruce, Nefertiti, and Karen Cairone. 2011. *Socially Strong, Emotionally Secure: 50 Activities to Promote Resilience in Young Children*. Lewisville, NC: Gryphon House.

Carr, Rachel. 1973. *Be a Frog, a Bird or a Tree*. New York: Doubleday.

Colker, Laura J., and Derry Koralek. 2019. *Making Lemonade: Teaching Young Children to Think Optimistically*. St. Paul, MN: Redleaf Press.

Cooper, Patricia M. 2017. "Vivian Paley's 'Pedagogy of Meaning': Helping Wild Things Grow Up to Be Garbage Men." In *Storytelling in Early Childhood: Enriching Language, Literacy and Classroom Culture*, edited by Teresa Cremin, Rosie Flewitt, Ben Mardell, and Joan Swann, 133–49. New York: Routledge.

Devereux Center for Resilient Children's website: *www.centerforresilientchildren.org*

Green, Jarrod. 2017. *I'm OK! Building Resilience through Physical Play*. St. Paul, MN: Redleaf Press.

Hafner, Mary Lynn. 2019. *The Joy of Movement: Lesson Plans and Large-Motor Activities for Preschoolers*. St. Paul, MN: Redleaf Press.

Haughey, Sally. 2020. *Wonder Art Workshop: Creative, Child-Led Experiences for Nurturing Imagination, Curiosity and a Love of Learning*. Beverly, MA: Quarto. See also her website: *www.fairydustteaching.com*

Heffron, Claire, and Lauren Drobnjak. 2019. *Playful Learning Lab for Kids: Whole-Body Sensory Adventures to Enhance Focus, Engagement, and Curiosity*. Beverly, MA: Quarto. See also their website: *www.theinspiredtreehouse.com*

Heroman, Cate. 2017. *Making and Tinkering with STEM: Solving Design Challenges with Young Children*. Washington, DC: National Association for the Education of Young Children.

Koch, Isabel. 1999. *Like a Fish in Water: Yoga for Children*. Rochester, VT: Inner Traditions.

Malenfant, Nicole. 2006. *Routines and Transitions: A Guide for Early Childhood Professionals*. St. Paul, MN: Redleaf Press.

Murphy, Lisa. 2009. *Ooey Gooey Tooey*. Rochester, NY: Ooey Gooey. See also her website: *www.ooeygooey.com*

Troupe, Thomas Kingsley. 2019. *Keep It Simple, Rapunzel*. North Mankato, MN: Capstone.

References

Ackerman, Robert J. 1987. *Children of Alcoholics: A Guide for Parents, Educators, and Therapists*. 2nd ed. New York: Learning Publications/Fireside.

American Academy of Pediatrics. 2014. *Adverse Childhood Experiences and the Lifelong Consequences of Trauma*. Itasca, IL: American Academy of Pediatrics. https://www.unitedforyouth.org/resources/adverse -childhood-experiences-and-the-lifelong-consequences-of-trauma.

American Medical Association. 2021. "Issue Brief: Nation's Drug-Related Overdose and Death Epidemic Continues to Worsen." www.ama-assn.org/system/files/issue-brief -increases-in-opioid-related-overdose.pdf.

American Psychiatric Association. 2013. *Diagnostic and Statistical Manual of Mental Disorders (DSM-5)*. Arlington, VA: American Psychiatric Publishing.

Blair, Clancy, and C. Cybele Raver. 2015. "School Readiness and Self-Regulation: A Developmental Psychobiological Approach." *Annual Review of Psychology* 66:711–31. http://doi.org/10.1146/annurev-psych-010814-015221.

Bodrova, Elena, Carrie Germeroth, and Deborah J. Leong. 2013. "Play and Self-Regulation: Lessons from Vygotsky." *American Journal of Play* 6 (1): 111–23.

Brazelton, T. Berry, and Joshua D. Sparrow. 2005. *Understanding Sibling Rivalry—The Brazelton Way*. Boston: Da Capo Lifelong Books, 2005.

Brown, Fraser. 2014. "The Healing Power of Play: Therapeutic Work with Chronically Neglected and Abused Children." *Children* 1 (3): 474–88.

Center on the Developing Child. 2011. *Building the Brain's "Air Traffic Control" System: How Early Experiences Shape the Development of Executive Function: Working Paper No. 11*. https://46y5eh11fhgw3ve3ytpwxt9r-wpengine.netdna-ssl.com/wp-content /uploads/2011/05/How-Early-Experiences-Shape-the-Development-of-Executive -Function.pdf.

——. 2016. *From Best Practices to Breakthrough Impacts: A Science-Based Approach to Building a More Promising Future for Young Children and Families*. Cambridge, MA: Center on the Developing Child at Harvard University. https://46y5eh11fhgw3ve3ytpwxt9r -wpengine.netdna-ssl.com/wp-content/uploads/2016/05/From_Best_Practices _to_Breakthrough_Impacts-4.pdf.

Cohen, Lynn E., and Sandra Waite-Stupiansky, eds. 2017. *Theories of Early Childhood Education: Developmental, Behaviorist and Critical.* New York: Routledge.

Compton, Michelle Kay, and Robin Chappelle Thompson. 2018. *StoryMaking: The Maker Movement Approach to Literacy for Early Learners.* St. Paul, MN: Redleaf Press.

———. 2020. *Makerspaces: Remaking Your Play and STEAM Early Learning Areas.* St. Paul, MN: Redleaf Press.

Conners-Burrow, Nicola A., Angela Kyzer, Joy Pemberton, Lorraine McKelvey, Leanne Whiteside-Mansell, and James Fulmer. 2013. "Child and Family Factors Associated with Teacher-Reported Behavior Problems in Young Children of Substance Abusers." *Child and Adolescent Mental Health* 18 (4): 218–24. https://doi.org/10.1111/camh.12010.

Diamond, Adele. 2014. "Executive Functions: Insights into Ways to Help More Children Thrive." *Zero to Three* 35 (2): 9–17.

Dombrink-Green, Megan. 2011. "A Conversation with Vivian Gussin Paley." *Young Children* 66 (5): 90–93.

Duckworth, Eleanor R. 2006. *"The Having of Wonderful Ideas" and Other Essays on Teaching and Learning.* 3rd ed. New York: Teachers College Press.

Eiden, Rina D., Craig Colder, Ellen P. Edwards, and Kenneth E. Leonard. 2009. "A Longitudinal Study of Social Competence among Children of Alcoholic and Nonalcoholic Parents: Role of Parental Psychopathology, Parental Warmth, and Self-Regulation." *Psychology of Addictive Behaviors* 23 (1): 36–46. https://doi.apa.org/doi/10.1037/a0014839.

Felitti, V. J., R. F. Anda, D. Nordenberg, D. F. Williamson, A. M. Spitz, V. Edwards, and J. S. Marks. 1998. "Relationship of Childhood Abuse and Household Dysfunction to Many of the Leading Causes of Death in Adults: The Adverse Childhood Experiences (ACE) Study." *American Journal of Preventive Medicine* 14 (4): 245–58.

Fleer, Marilyn, and Marie Hammer. 2013. "Emotions in Imaginative Situations: The Valued Place of Fairy Tales for Supporting Emotion Regulation." *Mind, Culture, and Activity* 20 (3): 240–59.

Friedman-Krauss, Allison, and Steven W. Barnett. 2013. *Early Childhood Education: Pathways to Better Health.* NIEER Policy Brief. New Brunswick, NJ: National Institute for Early Education Research.

Galinsky, Ellen. 2020. "Words Matter: Moving from Trauma-Informed Care to Asset-Informed Care." *Young Children* 75 (6): 46–55.

Gartrell, Dan, and Karen B. Cairone. 2014. "Fostering Resilience: Teaching Social-Emotional Skills." *Young Children* 69 (3): 92–93.

Grant, Bridget F., S. Patricia Chou, Tulshi D. Saha, Roger P. Pickering, Bradley T. Kerridge, June Ruan, and Deborah S. Hasin. 2017. "Prevalence of 12-Month Alcohol Use, High-Risk Drinking, and DSM-IV Alcohol Use Disorder in the United States, 2001–2002 to 2012–2013: Results from the National Epidemiologic Survey on Alcohol and Related Conditions." *JAMA Psychiatry* 74 (9): 911–23.

Green, Jarrod. 2017. *I'm OK! Building Resilience through Physical Play*. St. Paul, MN: Redleaf Press.

Harper Browne, Charlyn. 2014. "The Strengthening Families Approach and Protective Factors Framework: Branching Out and Reaching Deeper." Washington, DC: Center for the Study of Social Policy. https://cssp.org/wp-content/uploads/2018/11/Branching -Out-and-Reaching-Deeper.pdf.

Hearne, Betsy. 1993. *Beauties and Beasts*. Phoenix, AZ: Oryx.

Howell, Jacky, and Kimberly Reinhard, 2015. *Rituals and Traditions: Fostering a Sense of Community in Preschool*. Washington, DC: National Association for the Education of Young Children.

Lander, Laura, Janine Howsare, and Marilyn Byrne. 2013. "The Impact of Substance Use Disorders on Families and Children: From Theory to Practice." *Social Work in Public Health* 28 (3–4): 194–205.

LeBuffe, Paul A., and Jack Naglieri A. 2012. *Devereux Early Childhood Assessment for Preschoolers, Second Edition: User's Guide and Technical Manual*. Lewisville, NC: Kaplan Early Learning.

Lee, Trisha. 2016. *Princesses, Dragons and Helicopter Stories: Storytelling and Story Acting in the Early Years*. New York: Routledge.

Leong, Deborah J., and Elena Bodrova. 2012. "Assessing and Scaffolding: Make-Believe Play." *Young Children* 67 (1): 28–34.

Martin, Rafe. 1999. "Why Folktales?" *Storytelling Magazine*, January 1999. https://rafemartin.com/articles13.html.

Masten, Ann S. 2015. *Ordinary Magic: Resilience in Development*. New York: Guilford.

Moe, Jerry. 2019. "When a Child Grows Up with Addiction." Streamed live May 29, 2019. YouTube video, 17:10. https://youtu.be/hd7xh1OTUaI.

Murray, D. W., K. Rosanbalm, C. Christopoulos, and A. Hamoudi. 2015. *Self-Regulation and Toxic Stress: Foundations for Understanding Self-Regulation from an Applied Developmental Perspective*. OPRE Report #2015-21. Washington, DC: Office of Planning, Research and Evaluation, Administration for Children and Families, US Department of Health and Human Service.

National Institute on Drug Abuse (NIDA). 2021. Principles of Substance Abuse Prevention for Early Childhood. www.drugabuse.gov/publications /principles-substance-abuse-prevention-early-childhood /principles-substance-abuse-prevention-early-childhood.

National Scientific Council on the Developing Child. (2005) 2014. "Excessive Stress Disrupts the Architecture of the Developing Brain." Working Paper No. 3, updated ed. Cambridge, MA: National Scientific Council on the Developing Child. https://46y5eh11fhgw3ve3ytpwxt9r-wpengine.netdna-ssl.com/wp-content /uploads/2005/05/Stress_Disrupts_Architecture_Developing_Brain-1.pdf.

——. (2008) 2012. "Establishing a Level Foundation for Life: Mental Health Begins in Early Childhood." Working Paper No. 6. Cambridge, MA: National Scientific Council on the Developing Child. https://46y5eh11fhgw3ve3ytpwxt9r-wpengine.netdna-ssl.com/wp-content/uploads/2008/05/Establishing-a-Level-Foundation-for-Life-Mental-Health-Begins-in-Early-Childhood.pdf.

——. 2015. "Supportive Relationships and Active Skill-Building Strengthen the Foundations of Resilience." Working Paper No. 13. Cambridge, MA: National Scientific Council on the Developing Child. http://developingchild.harvard.edu/wp-content/uploads/2015/05/The-Science-of-Resilience.pdf.

Nicolopoulou, Ageliki, Kai S. Cortina, Hanle Ilgaz, Carolyn B. Cates, and Aline B. de Sá. 2015. "Using a Narrative- and Play-Based Activity to Promote Low-Income Preschoolers' Oral Language, Emergent Literacy, and Social Competence." *Early Childhood Research Quarterly* 31:147–62.

O'Connor, Cailin. 2020. "Protective Factors, ACES, HOPE and Resilience." Webinar presented March 4, 2020, Centers for Schools and Communities, Camp Hill, PA. https://vimeo.com/395510387.

Onchwari, Jacqueline. 2010. "Early Childhood Inservice and Preservice Teachers' Perceived Levels of Preparedness to Handle Stress in Their Students." *Early Childhood Education Journal* 37 (5): 391–400.

Paley, Vivian Gussin. 1984. *Boys and Girls: Superheroes in the Doll Corner*. Chicago: University of Chicago Press.

——. 1988. *Bad Guys Don't Have Birthdays: Fantasy Play at Four*. Chicago: University of Chicago Press.

——. 1990. *The Boy Who Would Be a Helicopter: The Uses of Storytelling in the Classroom*. Cambridge, MA: Harvard University Press.

——. 1992. *You Can't Say You Can't Play*. Cambridge, MA: Harvard University Press.

——. 1997. *The Girl with the Brown Crayon*. Cambridge, MA: Harvard University Press.

——. 2001. *In Mrs. Tully's Room: A Childcare Portrait*. Cambridge, MA: Harvard University Press.

——. 2004. *A Child's Work: The Importance of Fantasy Play*. Chicago: University of Chicago Press.

——. 2009. "The Importance of Fantasy, Fairness, and Friendship in Children's Play: An Interview with Vivian Gussin Paley." *American Journal of Play* 2 (2): 121–38.

——. 2010. *The Boy on the Beach: Building Community through Play*. Chicago: University of Chicago Press.

Piaget, Jean. 1962. *Play, Dreams and Imitation in Childhood*. New York: Norton.

——. 1965. *The Moral Judgment of the Child*. New York: Free Press.

Ronel, Natti, and Maayan Levy-Cahana. 2011. "Growing-Up with a Substance-Dependent Parent: Development of Subjective Risk and Protective Factors." *Substance Use & Misuse* 46 (5): 608–19. https://doi.org/10.3109/10826084.2010.527417.

Smith, Jeremy Adam. 2016. "The Science of Story." *Greater Good Magazine.* http://greatergood.berkeley.edu/article/item/science_of_the_story.

Solis, Jessica M., Julia M. Shadur, Alison R. Burns, and Andrea M. Hussong. 2012. "Understanding the Diverse Needs of Children Whose Parents Abuse Substances." *Current Drug Abuse Reviews* 5 (2): 135–47.

Tolkien, J. R. R. 1965. *Tree and Leaf.* Boston: Houghton-Mifflin.

Volkow, Nora D., K. D. Janda, E. Nestler, and A. Levine. 2014. "The Craving Brain: Neuroscience of Uncontrollable Urges." In *World Science Festival.* Symposium conducted at the World Science Festival in New York City. www.youtube.com/watch?v=p0lL1MN2yCs&feature=youtu.be.

Volkow, Nora D., and George Koob. 2015. "Brain Disease Model of Addiction: Why Is It So Controversial?" *Lancet Psychiatry* 2 (8): 677–79.

Vygotsky, Lev. 1978. *Mind in Society: The Development of Higher Psychological Processes.* Cambridge, MA: Harvard University Press.

Wineberg, Lenore P. 2020. "The Magic of Oral Storytelling." *Exchange* 42 (1) (January/February): 76–78.

Yolen, Jane. (1981) 2005. *Touch Magic: Fantasy, Faerie and Folklore in the Literature of Childhood.* New York: Philomel Books.

Index